MW01487725

# Feedback

*"Excellent books and research! Thanks for what you are doing."*

*"The book was excellent. Not too long and not too short either and your research was particularly very good."*

*"Time was not available during the 2010 expedition to apply the SeaBotix* (Corporation's Remotely Operated Vehicle) *ROV technology to the McMoneagle hypothesis, but if and when TIGHAR gets back to the island for more deep-water searching, I hope such a test will be included in the research plan."*

Tom King, PhD. - Senior Archaeologist - The International Group for Historic Aircraft Recovery (TIGHAR).

*"Received your book yesterday and thought I'd look at it briefly as I had things to do. But once I opened it, I kept reading it. Amazing ...fascinating"*

*"I have read the book and will now read it again more slowly to take it all in. I thought it was great. I know a lot of the background to RV and it ticks all the boxes, and the level of detail given by Joe M was amazing. The Princess Diana work was intriguing. The Amelia Earhart session(s) were great."*

*"Mr. McMoneagle has a proven track record and I am more inclined to favour his report. I hope he eventually receives feedback on the target."*

*"Interesting information. The quality of the investigation appears to be good. I very much appreciate the information from Joe McMoneagle."*

*"The book is fact filled with numerous illustrations and maps and I liked reading it very much. Well worth it`s price and I am most certainly going to read it again."*

TIGHAR's Executive Director, *"Ric* (Gillespie) *is utterly dismissive of paranormal powers as displayed by anyone but his remarkable horse Gofer. Others in the organization (This one, at least) are not so ready to reject alternative views of reality."*

Tom King, PhD. - Senior Archaeologist, the TIGHAR Group

# The Quick Take

Authority to award the Legion of Merit Medal is reserved for general officers and flag officers in pay grade O-9 (e.g., Lieutenant General and Vice Admiral) and above... Wikipedia.org

At least two witnesses must submit seven military forms for consideration as to the proper award. Based on the quality of the information, the military's Decorations Personnel selected the medal with the following prerequisites:

*The award is given for service rendered in a clearly exceptional manner. For service not related to actual war the term "key individual" applies to a narrower range of positions than in time of war and requires evidence of significant achievement. In peace-time, service should be in the nature of a special requirement or of an extremely difficult duty performed in an unprecedented and clearly exceptional manner.*

The U.S. Army's Legion of Merit Medal bestowal prerequisites.

Based on the quality of the information, these Military operations wanted Joseph McMoneagle's services:

*During his career, Mr. McMoneagle has provided ...informational support to the Central Intelligence Agency (CIA), Defense Intelligence Agency (DIA), National Security Agency (NSA), Drug Enforcement Agency (DEA), the Secret Service, Federal Bureau of Investigation (FBI), Immigration and Customs Enforcement (ICE), the National Security Council (NSC), most major commands (Army, Navy, Air Force, Intelligence) within the Department of Defense (DOD), and hundreds of other individuals, companies, and corporations.*

Paragraph from Mr. McMoneagle's CV.

# Evidential Details Mystery Series

Decorated United States Military Intelligence Psychic
Remote Viewer solves some of History's Greatest Mysteries

U.S. Legion of Merit Medal

# Amelia Earhart
## Take Off To Oblivion

Seeds/McMoneagle

©2021

The Logistics News Network, LLC. Chicago, Illinois

# Medals Received

Legion of Merit          Meritorious Service

# Citations

Meritorious Service with **one** Oak Leaf Cluster;[1]
Army Commendation with **two** Oak Leaf Clusters, Presidential Unit;
Meritorious Unit with **three** Oak Leaf Clusters;
Vietnam Gallantry Cross with Palm for gathering enemy intelligence for
Allied counter offensives.

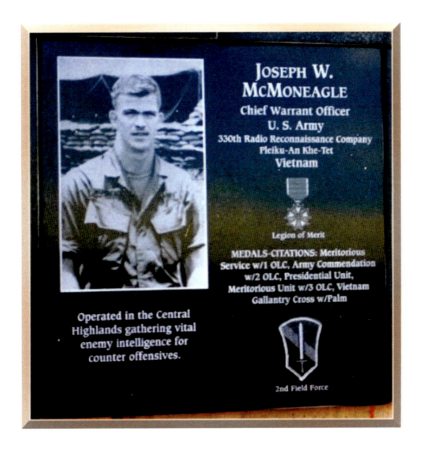

# The Bronze Commemorative Plaque on the Brick Wall

In what is clearly the most fascinating component of U.S. Military History, Joseph McMoneagle is the only man to be awarded medals for consistent accuracy in Remote Viewing (Psy-functioning) by a military. As *Operation Star Gate's* Number 1 Military Intelligence asset, he was the Pentagon's go to man when secret data could not be obtained by any other means or was time sensitive.

Published on the Evidential Details
Imprint, a Division of
Logistics News Network, LLC

# The Evidential Details Mysteries Series

Remote Viewing Session Work ©1998 All rights reserved
Updated Edition ©2021 by Logistics News Network, llc.
*Amelia Earhart – Take off to Oblivion* includes biographical references.

ISBN: 978-0-9826928-0–6
Library of Congress Card Number:  2010904602

- United States – Aeronautics – Flight - Aviation
- Amelia Earhart (1897-1937) – Fred Noonan - Aviation – World Flights – Ann Holtgren Pellegreno – The International Group for Historic Aircraft Recovery – University of Hawaii (HURL) – Phoenix International Corp. – Purdue University – Google 3D -  N.O.A.A. – U.K. Hydrographic Office
- U.S. Military Intelligence - Operation Stargate - McMoneagle, Joseph – Puthoff PhD., Dr. Harold E. – Remote Viewing – Stanford Research Institute – Neurophysiology - Anomalous Cognition

Book design by LNN, llc.
Printed in the United States of America

If you want to contact us, or are unable to purchase this book, or our other fine history books in your local bookstore, visit our web site at: **www.EvidentialDetails.com**

**Note:** Any interpretations or historical conclusions contained herein cannot be considered to represent the opinion of, or to be endorsed by, Joseph McMoneagle or any other individual. The final manuscript was not submitted for review. There was no prior knowledge of when the manuscript was to be made available or the medium this research would be brought forward. Pictures on the Internet continue to be a problem for all concerned. It remains an effort where one can only strive to be correct. In the event of inaccurate credit. Please contact us with the corrected information and proof of ownership. Word *only* portions, of this book may be repro-duced for academic dissertations or in non-fiction works within lawfully established Fair Use guidelines with proper crediting. No text may be altered.

Amelia Earhart

# Table of Contents

The Quick Take……..............................................................……....4

Medals………................................................................…...…...…..6

Acknowledgment…...........................................................………...10

Preface…........................................................…...........…...…......11

**Introduction** - Introduction to remote viewing targeting the late Princess
Diana Spencer's 1997 auto accident……........................................….13

## Part II

**Target** – Amelia Earhart's Last Flight….....................................…43
   The Evidence……………...........................…...…......………80
    Aftermath…........................................................………..83

**Section II**…......................................................……..............……91
    The Atoll's Enigma……………......................……............…..95
    Third Party Validators…………........................…............…..112
    Theater Rain…......................................……............……...113
    Interpretive Ambiguity…............................................…......121
    To the Debris Field………………......................…............…124
    Bibliography………….........…......…............……...............…126

## Part III

Incredible Credentials…………......................................…...…......128

The Military's "Human Use" Clearances Conflict…...................................130

Encounters with the Chinese RV Program..................................…….....131

The Army's Remote Viewing Project Protocols.....................…..........…….133

Program Beginnings - Director Harold E. Puthoff, PhD.........................138

The Remote Viewers Military Bookshelf…...............................................154

Additional Taskings…...............................................................….......156

End Notes…………...........................................................…….........158

# ACKNOWLEDGEMENT

The author would like to acknowledge the hours spent by Joseph McMoneagle. He is a peerless individual in the world and will always be understood as an exceptional scientific pioneer into the possibilities of the human brain. I want to thank all the others in the original military unit that I have met, or corresponded with, telephoned, studied under or shook their hands.

I would like to thank Ann Holtgren Pellegreno for her recollections, pictures and support. He was the first woman to replicate Earhart's world flight in an Electra 10 on the 30th anniversary (1967). She will always be remembered as an authentication of women's abilities and "can do" spirit.

I would like to mention the people who work so hard to put the July Amelia Earhart Birthplace Museum Festival together every year in Atchison, Kansas.

I would like to acknowledge the people of the Monroe Institute™ whose pioneering programs help people expand the possibilities of human consciousness.

And then, to all the wonderful and truly fascinated people, of every persuasion, whose judgment it was that this series of books be brought forward.

# PREFACE

With the August, 1998 receipt of the narrative and maps, this target was intended to support those already involved with the Earhart mystery. Instead, we ran into negativity, some publishing restraint of trade and suddenly Festival interference after a decade of attendance. This is because this book is what insiders considered to be the mystery's answer. The problem was that the result would reduce Earhart's "mystoric" value – hence County revenue. Systemic hostility was subsequently confirmed by the Atchison Chamber of Commerce's demeanor. There is money in mystery and diminishing Atchison's marginal take from their annual Amelia Earhart Birthplace Museum Festival revenues could not be tolerated. No other author has this suppression problem.

All of this was brought to an unethical level with this book's Internet ratings. Book evaluation critics at both *Good Reads* and *Bookwire* rated this book a five (5) star read – a difficult accolade to achieve. Then it was removed from the web sites to hinder sales. The Castaways theory has no such opposition as it is mystery protection. We support the festival and the people of Atchison, KS, but our mystery solving capability remains unique.

Elsewhere, to read material on the origins of the military's involvement with Remote Viewing, kindly refer to our **Beginnings** section displayed in the Table of Contents. Our Princess Diana Spencer **Introduction** was designed to provide new information, highlight some remote viewing nomenclature while demonstrating military intelligence's level of viewer integrity.

For any researcher, it is the guarded realization that you have connected unattainable investigational dots that is the most intellectually stimulating factor in any horizon field of inquiry. Verifying those details confirmed the viability of Remote Viewing as a tool when used in conjunction with other research sources.

What I can say is that I have been involved with the most fascinating process of historical inquiry ever. As likely the only author to conduct historic research backward - with the unsolvable solution in hand - I came to call those conformational dots the *Evidential Details*.

Chicago – 2021

# Inside the Military Intelligence Program known as Operation Star Gate

We tried a lot of things. Like I always tell everyone, we "improved" on the Ingo (Swann) method a thousand times in a thousand ways. But our bottom line always had to be accuracy, so we had to keep track of the improvements. Most of those times, the resulting data showed that the end result of our "improvements" was to have the accuracy drop down and down and down. Those things which proved over time to work, we kept.

Ingo will be the first to tell you that what we did and taught to new people coming into the unit wasn't his "pure" method. The minute someone would come back from Ingo's training, we would try to see if there was some way to make what they had learned work better in a military / political / espionage setting. Some things did work, and they are now incorporated into the "military" method which passes for the Ingo Swann method.[1]

E-mail from Leonard Buchanan – 7/29/98
Former Data Base Manager for Operation Star Gate

---

[1] The late Ingo Swann was the original psy-experimenter for the U.S. Intelligence and Security Command (INSCOM) and developed the protocols for remote viewing sessions and training.

Amelia Earhart

Our

# Introduction
## To Remote Viewing

A Review of the terminology,
history, and capabilities targeting

## The Former Princess of Wales Diana Spencer's 1997 Auto Accident

(For the **cover story**, please refer to the Table of Contents)

"*When they* (University researchers) *did produce an incredibly accurate response during an experiment, it was in even a moderate sense "unnerving." In a greater sense, it was "earth shattering." As* (Stanford PhD) *Russell* (Targ) *implied, for some it was even "terrifying". In no case, was it ever taken lightly, as it always had a tendency to alter one's perspective towards reality and/or our place within it.*"

~ Medals Recipient Joseph W. McMoneagle~

# Evidential Details

It was the peak of the Twentieth Century's Cold War 1945-1990]. The United States, the old Soviet Union, and the People's Republic of China were striving to find new ways to get an intelligence edge. During the years 1968 to 1972, the United States obtained reports that scientists in the Soviet Union had had some success with a telekinesis program that introduced atrial fibulation into frog hearts causing a heart attack. Realizing the program could target key military and political leaders, and so driven by a threat assessment, the Central Intelligence Agency funded the Stanford Research Institute (SRI) think tank in Menlo Park, California to conduct an analysis about what humanity through the ages has pondered. The doctors were to determine scientifically if psy-functioning could be taught, quantified and directed using written protocols. If so, did this represent a credible threat to the people of the United States or NATO? Their highly classified "Black Ops" program lasted from early 1972 until November 1995.

Under the most extensive and stringent experimentation two PhD's could devise, the SRI, supported by other labs and the U.S. Army, developed mankind's first "psychic" protocols. "This led to greater understanding of everything from methods of evaluation, to establishing statistical standards, to how a human brain might be appropriately studied."[i] When their findings went public, many in the academic community were privately stunned.

Eventually this covert military effort focused on real world data collection. As the years of research, analysis and application moved through the 1970's and 80's, some Army brass, with wholly personal motives, would attempt to quash the program even when research costs did not affect their budget. "All the funding had been approved on a year-to-year basis, and only then based on how effective the unit was in supporting the tasking agencies. These reviews were made semi-annually at the Senate and House select subcommittee level, where the work results were reviewed within the context in which it was happening."[ii]

Fortunately, for The People, the program was given different code names and moved around various defense budgets until much of the research and development was completed. What emerged was an incredibly "robust" database - and a process - referred to as Controlled Remote Viewing [CRV].

Much of the work took place within the 902nd United States Army Intelligence Group at Fort Meade, Maryland, whose barracks have been demolished. However, from the fastidiously maintained database emerged statistically advanced practitioners; world-class viewers whose RV data was the "best in the business." Among these, one remote viewer was the first in history to be decorated with the Army's Legion of Merit and Meritorious Service Awards (with five Oak Leaf Clusters) for having made key contributions to the Intelligence community. This individual was tasked to unlock the mysteries in this Evidential Details Book Series.

Obviously, accuracy is the name of the game. As with any horizon application process, purposefully moving the human brain into a sub-quark quantum mechanics level required new clinical terminology. As the CRV process was tested, protocols written and cautiously modified, scientists documented mental hazards to accuracy. These hindrances were cataloged and their characteristics differentiated. Year after year laboratory research determined accurate mental representations could be inhibited in a variety of ways. Some of these mental distracters included:

**Physical Inclemency** - Knowledge of an expected disruption like a phone call or someone about to arrive during a remote viewing session.

**Advanced Visuals** - A fleeting thought you cannot get rid of before a session.

**Emotional Distracters or Attractors** - An image you do or do not want to view regardless of the tasking.

**Front Loading** - Knowledge of what the target is before the viewing session. If localized, it can be used in targeting a feature within the whole picture, perhaps a house in a meadow in front of a mountain. However, without neutral wording like "The target is man-made" the object is generally rendered unworkable.

**Analytic Overlay** [AOL] - If a viewer is not informed about the target and not front-loaded but still has personal information about it, that knowledge may pollute the information stream rendering the session unworkable. Analytic Overlay can be a problem for any viewer. According to the military's former #1 remote viewer:

**Joseph McMoneagle - Analytic overlay - CRV** [Controlled Remote Viewing]**, as a format or method for learning remote viewing, offers a structure within which you can discard or identify specific elements within a session for which you are certain or not certain. Analytic Over-Lay (AOL) being a common label for something that falls within the "uncertain"**

category. However, when studied (under laboratory conditions), there is evidence that fifty percent of the time, information labeled as AOL actuality, wasn't.

I have observed just as many times, someone being smacked up against the side of the head while attempting CRV because they had strayed from the given format and slipped into AOL. I think that sometimes you may forget that CRV was developed within the hallowed halls of SRI and was taught there for years. I saw very little difference in the AOL pitfalls with CRV and other methodologies. I did see that to some extent it was a highly polished technique, which was more easily transferred through training.

With this quick overview of the subconscious transference of recollections, we turn to the remote viewing of the Princess Diana Spencer's accident in the early morning hours of August 31, 1997. As this researcher found, how one targets is critical to the result. In the fall of 1997, the massive press coverage of Princess Diana's accident and funeral emerged as a very real overlay problem. There had been much less news coverage at the hotel, so the Hotel Ritz in Paris, France, rather than the crash site, was targeted. At the time, this event was less than two months old. No accident report had been completed. Upon request, an envelope, with a second target envelope inside, was mailed to Joseph McMoneagle's home with nothing more than targeting coordinates and a date. A skeptical *Life Magazine* reporter was also on hand.

The viewing event started at 11:49 am on October 29, 1997. What makes these sessions interesting is that the reader can sense the Intelligence intellect. Having viewed 1200 targets in just the last two years of the military's Operation Star Gate alone, McMoneagle was the only viewer to participate in the program for twenty-three years. **Target Envelope No. 102997 - (no additional information other than what's sealed within the envelope.)**

\* \* \*

As her size nine shoes hit the airport tarmac the former Princess of Wales Diana Spencer, 36, knew she was entitled to an escort by that special branch of the French Interior Ministry charged with guarding visiting dignitaries - the Service de Protection des Hautes Personalities (SPHP). But there would be no need of the service once she left the airport. This was to be a private visit.

Diana was returning from a Mediterranean yachting vacation off Northeast Sardinia. She and Emad "Dodi" Al-Fayed, [1955-1997] had been aboard the Fayed family's $27 million dollar (US$44.5m/2020), 195 foot yacht *Jonikal,* with 16 crewmembers.

At this point, "…in her relationship with Dodi Fayed she was displaying a new facet. In some ways a late developer, she had grown up and was simply having some adult fun."[iii] But the couple had been stalked by high-speed paparazzi boats wherever they went. On their last afternoon, they came ashore at the Cala de Volpe in Sardinia and the, "Paparazzi swarmed around them like bees, flashing away."[iv] Forced back to the boat, "Things came to a head when a scuffle broke out between three paparazzi and several members of the *Jonikal*'s crew."[v]

At about the same time, hundreds of miles away, a 73 year-old grandfather, Edward Williams, entered the police station in Mountain Ash, Mid Glamorgan, Wales. He reported that he had had a premonition that Princess Diana was going to die. The police log, time stamped 14:12 hours on August 27, 1997, stated:

*"He* [Williams] *said he was a psychic and predicted that Princess Diana was going to die. In previous years he has predicted that the Pope and Ronald Reagan were going to be the victims of assassination. On both occasions he was proven to be correct. Mr. Williams appeared to be quite normal."*[vi]

Based on his previous record the police passed this report along to the department's Special Branch Investigative Unit.

Fed up with the non-stop press hassle, on Saturday August 30, Dodi and Diana boarded the Fayed's Gulfstream IV jet at Olbia airport in Sardinia and flew north. They arrived at Le Bourget Airport about 10 miles north of Paris, France at 3:20 p.m. Fayed's butler Rene Delorm recalled, "Unfortunately, we had a welcoming committee of about ten paparazzi waiting for us."[vii] About 600 feet (183 meters) away was a Mercedes and a Range Rover. "We had all seen the paparazzi, so we moved quickly. We wanted to get out of the plane and into the cars as fast as possible. (Body Guard) Trevor (Rees-Jones) was the first out of the jet…"[viii]

The entourage had a police escort from the airport up to France's highway A-1 leading to Paris. But as they entered the expressway, reporter's cars and two man motorcycle teams immediately dogged the entourage. The paparazzi were armed with powerful, maximum strength, flashes to penetrate deep into the car. Philippe Dourneau, 35, was Dodi's chauffeur. But in the Range Rover vehicle there had been an unexplained switch. At the wheel was the Assistant Chief of Hotel Security Henri Paul. It is unclear why Paul was chauffeuring that afternoon and not at the Ritz Hotel as acting Security Chief.

Once on the highway, Dodi instructed Ritz Hotel driver Dourneau to pick up speed in an attempt to elude photographers. What ensued was a high-speed pursuit with motorcycle cameramen weaving in and out shooting pictures. The motorcycle whirl was so intense Diana reportedly cried out in alarm that someone could get killed.[ix]

The photographer's strategy was to slow the convoy down. "Then a black car sped ahead of us and ducked in front of the Mercedes, braking and making us slow down so the paparazzi on motorcycles could get more pictures. They were risking their lives and ours, just to get a shot of Dodi and Diana riding in a car. "*Unbelievable*", exclaimed butler Rene Delorm.[x]

Dodi was not accustomed to this and after their high seas harassment, his patience was running thin. Pursuing for miles, the paparazzi then used phones to notify photographers ahead to form another gauntlet on the next highway segment. The Fayed cars split up in an attempt to divide the photographers. Some pursued Henri Paul as he drove to Dodi's apartment to deliver the luggage.

Finally, their Mercedes made it to Bois de Boulogne on the outskirts of Paris to visit the Fayed's Windsor Villa. They arrived about 3:45 p.m. Then they were off to the Ritz Hotel in downtown Paris at 4:35. Alerted by the cameramen the hotel entrance was by now packed with photographers which in turn generated curiosity seekers in the general public.

Once inside the hotel, Diana checked into the second floor Imperial Suite and went to have her hair done. She also made some phone calls. After the accident, London's *Daily Mail* correspondent Richard Kay stated that Diana had called him saying she was going to complete her contractual obligations through November and then go into private life.

Another call was made to psychic Rita Rogers whom Diana had been in contact with since 1994. Just three weeks earlier, on

August 12, Dodi and Di had visited Rogers for a reading on Dodi. She warned him not to go driving in Paris. *"I saw a tunnel, motorcycles, there was this tremendous sense of speed."*[xi] Uneasy, Rogers reminded Diana about her readout concerning a Parisian tunnel saying, *"...remember what I told Dodi."*[xii]

At seven o'clock, they left the hotel for Dodi's apartment at Rue 1 Arsene-Houssaye arriving at 7:15 p.m. Here the couple found the street so crowded they could not even open the car door. "The paparazzi literally mobbed the couple," said (32 year old former Royal Marine Kes) Wingfield. "They really disturbed and frightened the Princess, even though she was used to this. These paparazzi were shouting, which made them even more frightening. I had to push them back physically.'"[xiii] Butler Rene recalled:

*"...I could see they were being mobbed. I heard the shouting, saw the flashes going off and watched a security guard shove one of the photographers. Dodi did his best to shield Diana as Trevor and Kes fought to clear a path to the door... The princess was ashen and trembling, and Dodi was angry as they stalked through the apartment door..."*[xiv]

This was the way it was going to be. Rumors were rife about a marriage proposal and some wealthy publishers made it clear big money was available to the photographer that got the "million dollar shot". But no million dollars had been budgeted.

Later, things settled down, and Dodi had returned from shopping for two rings at the Repossi Jewelry Boutique, Rene recounted, "I met Dodi as he walked through the kitchen doorway, his eyes gleaming with excitement. It was then that he showed me the ring. *'Make sure we have champagne on ice when we come back from dinner,'* he told me urgently. *'I'm going to propose to her tonight!'"*[xv] Elated, he also phoned this proposal news to his cousin Hassan Yassin that evening.[xvi] [2]

Dodi had the Hotel staff book a 9:45 p.m. dinner reservation at the fashionable restaurant Chez Benoit on the Rue Saint Martin. He also phoned the Ritz staff he would not be returning. As a result, Henri Paul departed for the weekend at 7:05p.m.

At 9:30 p.m., Dodi and Diana left the apartment for dinner but could not get through the crowd at the restaurant entrance. It was clear they could not enter a restaurant together. The

---

[2] Dodi received a US$100,000/month ($164.915/2020) allowance from his father.

enormous number of paparazzi forced Dodi to cancel their arrangements. The Press was controlling his special night with this special lady. A frustrated Dodi decided they should make the four mile drive to the Hotel Ritz where they could dine in France's only "safe" restaurant. But Henri Paul had gone for the weekend and the abrupt change in plans left the hotel staff with no time to prepare for their arrival.

When they arrived at the Ritz, another press riot broke out. It took Diana two whole minutes to negotiate the camera gauntlet the 20 feet from the front door drive-up to the hotel turnstile. The security camera time stamped her entrance at 9:53 p.m. Security man Wingfield said:

*"I had to protect her physically from the paparazzi, who were coming really too close to her[.] Their cameras were right next to her face."*[xvii]

Furious, Dodi started shouting at his employees about no security to shield the 10-second walk up from the driveway. Shaken, the press savvy Diana wept in the lobby. Everyone was upset. With the owner's son angry, and the security force completely embattled, a decision was made to call the Security Chief back to work. Francois Tendil called Henri Paul's cell phone at 9:55 p.m.

Once safely in their room, Dodi called his father Mohammed Al-Fayed at approximately 10:00 p.m. He said the two would announce their engagement the next week when Diana returned from England.[xviii] "Diana always had the children for the last few days before they went back to school at the start of a new term, so that she could get everything ready and make sure they had the right kit."[xix] On Friday, she had called to confirm her boys would be at the airport to meet her on Sunday morning.

Dinner was ordered from the hotel's Imperial Suite restaurant. Diana's last meal was scrambled eggs with mushrooms and asparagus, then vegetable tempura with fillet of sole. As Di and Dodi were trying to dine normally, Henri Paul pushed his way back into the hotel through the lurking paparazzi.

For this targeting, the Hotel Ritz Building was tasked using the proper date, time, and location coordinates. As McMoneagle looked at a double blind envelope on his dining table, he started:

**McMoneagle - I find myself standing next to a man who is inside some kind of a public building. He is approxi-**

mately five feet, ten inches in height, good build, good condition physically. He weighs about 165 pounds, is clean shaven, light brown hair, right handed, 38-40 years of age, and is not British or American; meaning he probably has another language other than English as his native tongue. [3]

Upon his return, Henri Paul waited around the Ritz for about two hours. He allegedly had a couple drinks at the bar. The Ritz security cameras recorded his behavior, which would be used for future analysis. As Chief of Security, he was certainly aware of their placement and recording capabilities.

McMoneagle - Building interior - Where he (Paul) is within the building is inside of a very elaborate corridor. It runs the full length of the building and has lots of gilded paint, mirrors, thick carpets, lots of flowers, and is very fancy.

The corridor runs straight out to a front entry which is well lit and very busy (even though my sense is that it is very late at night). There is an area off to the right of this corridor which has a lot of dark paneling and dark colors with a long bar or type of counter. So, this may be the reception area of the hotel or something like that.

Where he (Paul) is standing is where the main corridor intersects with a short corridor that runs off at a ninety degree angle to the left. It intersects with some kind of a smaller staff or receiving area; perhaps a back door to the building. It is recessed and that is where his car is parked.

The Etoile Limousine Company manager Jean-Francis Musa, 39, provided six luxury cars to the Ritz Hotel for their exclusive use. This Mercedes was licensed as a Grande Remise auto meaning only a licensed chauffeur was authorized to drive it. Henri Paul did not have those credentials.

McMoneagle - Driver - I believe that he (Paul) drives a cab or limo...on the side, because I associate him with a car, which is parked outside and he is thinking about this car, or it seems to occupy his thoughts for some reason. He is mostly interested with driving from point A to point B. I believe he is not alone and get a strong feeling of mixed male/female in

---

[3] Paul was 167 lbs. and he was 41 years old. He had brown hair and was also balding. His native tongue was French. He spoke fluent English and some German.

energy; which either means his passenger will be gay, or consist of two people--a male and a female.

Limo is not a stretch limo but a short, black and formal kind of car. I get an impression of a Mercedes emblem or some kind of emblem like that,[4] so I'm assuming it is a very expensive car, could be a Mercedes. It is formal and black with an extended foot space in the back seat. Four doors. It is very heavy and my sense is that it might be equipped for hardened tires, etc.; which leads me to believe that at least one of the passengers [Trevor Rees-Jones, 29] might be a bodyguard [but] this may be Analytic overlay caused by the excessive feelings of security surrounding this vehicle and driver.

* * *

Information about Henri Paul's mixed motivations have come to light in the years since the accident. Born one of five brothers on July 3, 1956 in the port town of Lorient, France, he had a Bachelors Degree in Mathematics and Science from the Lycee St. Louis and had won several contests for his skill as a classical pianist. He became a pilot in 1976 but was unable to qualify as a jet fighter pilot when he joined the French Air Force in 1979. Paul did however achieve the rank of Lieutenant while assigned to Security in the French Air Force Reserves.

In 1986, Paul helped setup Ritz Security. He went on to become Assistant Director. On the day of the accident, he was carrying 12,560 francs (US$2,280/$3760/2020) and his savings account pass-book.[5] Where the money came from is unknown, but he was one of only two men in France that had access to the automobile conversations of Dodi and Di. The ability to advise the press of their plans would have been of great value.

Personal adversity. Henry Paul had recently been passed over for promotion a second time by Hotel Ritz management. The first disappointment had come on Jan 1, 1993 when the nod went

---

[4] The Mercedes S 280 sedan, valued at about $100,000 (US$164.915/2020) was engineered with eight advanced safety systems. The car had a reinforced chassis and roof. It had energy absorbing front and rear end crumple zones with electronic traction control. It also had an electronic ESP sensing system, which monitored trajectory with wheel speed to sense cornering speeds.

5 Henri Paul's salary was US$40,000 ($65,965/2020) per year.

to colleague Jean Hocquet even though Paul was obviously in position as the number two security man. Now again, effective June 30, 1997, as "Deputy Chief" he became the defacto head of a twenty person security team while Ritz Management searched for another chief. Now economically vulnerable, Paul had been informed of this exactly one month before the accident.

Post mortem tests stated Paul had consumed two anti-depressants called Fluoxetine and Tiapride before the accident. Fluoxetine is the active ingredient in Prozac and together these drugs are commonly used to fight alcoholism. When alcohol is introduced, the intoxicant effect is multiplied. On September 17, a different laboratory's final report was issued. It stated that Henri Paul had been in, *"moderate chronic alcoholism for a minimum of one week."*[xx] Once this became public, the Ritz's attorneys and Mohammed Al-Fayed found themselves on the defensive. An unlicensed employee now appeared criminally negligent in a multiple wrongful death accident while in Hotel Ritz employ. It now became negligent death vs. the Al-Fayeds.

France's intoxication limit is 0.50 grams per liter. One lab report stated Henri Paul's blood alcohol level was 1.87 g/l. This was the equivalent drinking eight or nine shots of whiskey in what was found to be an empty stomach. The Paris Prosecutor's Office Report stated:

*"On this particular point, numerous expert's reports examined following the autopsy on the body of Henri Paul rapidly showed the presence of a level of pure alcohol per litre of blood of between 1.73 and 1.75 grams, which is far superior, in all cases, than the legal level.*

*Similarly, these analyses revealed as [did] those carried out on samples of the hair and bone marrow of the deceased, that he regularly consumed Prozac and Tiapridal, both medicines which are not recommended for drivers, as they provoke a change in the ability to be vigilant, particularly when they are taken in combination with alcohol."*[xxi]

So had Henri Paul been out drinking? He had returned to the Ritz two hours and fifty minutes after departing. But no one knew where he was or what he was doing when he received the Ritz phone call. Subsequent investigations about who had seen Paul during this period failed to provide a single witness. In Paris, in the fall of 1997, there was a real fear of liability for anyone acknowledging Paul had been drinking in their establishment.

Nonetheless, the French media reported "*someone*" saw Paul drinking "aperitifs" between 7:05 and 10:08 p.m. that evening. "Someone" is wide open. But it means that after he got the urgent call to return at 9:55 p.m., he dallied almost another quarter-hour before departing which is hard to believe given the tone of the call. This was unsatisfactory. The critical question about what Paul was doing, before returning to the hotel, remains unknown.

**McMoneagle - I think he was in fact sitting in a small restaurant or coffee shop, very near where he lives. Maybe even on the corner near his house. He was alone as far as I can tell. I think he was in fact drinking coffee. I do not think he was depressed, at least not more than usual. Also, regardless of what might be said, I DID NOT get a sense that he was drunk. It is remotely possible that he was taking some kind of a medication but I doubt it.**

Coffee! Not drunk! This flew in the face of the formal investigation. Months before this controversy started, we were privately aware Henri Paul was not drunk.

Henri Paul was a pilot. Research indicated it was impossible to reconcile allegations of alcoholism with Paul's recent physical examination. Unbeknownst to the authorities issuing the report, just two days before the accident, Paul had completed a "rigorous" physical examination to renew his pilot's license. His *Certificat D'Aptitude Physique et Mentale* showed, "No signs of alcoholism."[xxii] A direct medical conflict supporting McMoneagle. Was Paul really fighting alcoholism? Six months after these sessions, the Ritz Hotel security videos further reaffirmed our data.

Behavioral Psychologist Dr. Martin Skinner commented in Fulcrum Productions documentary for ITV. The doctor stated there were no behavioral signs of drunkenness as Henri Paul waited for Dodi and Diana.

**Skinner**: *I don't think there is evidence, from the video, that can suggest he looked drunk. The pictures of him walking up and down the corridor are straight and smooth. He is standing very still and there is nothing in his demeanor, from these videos, to suggest that there are any problems with his competence in this situation.*[xxiii]

Next came a statement from Trevor Rees-Jones, the front

seat bodyguard sitting next to Paul. About intoxication, he said:

**Rees-Jones**: *I had no reason to suspect he was drunk. He did not look or sound like he had been drinking. He just seemed his normal self. He was working. He was competent. End of story. I can state quite categorically that he was not a hopeless drunk as some have tried to suggest. I like to think I have enough intelligence to see if the guy was plastered or not – and he wasn't.*[xxiv]

Neither the bodyguards, nor Dodi, or anyone else at the Hotel detected anything unusual in Paul's behavior. But there was more. Paul's blood was next reported as containing abnormally high carbon monoxide levels - twenty percent too much. How this happened has never been determined. But doctors agree it is impossible for a forty-year-old man, with that much poison in his blood stream, not to look and feel sick - too sick for high speed urban driving. When the press advanced the idea car exhaust was the source of Paul's poisoning, Dodi's father, Mohammed Al-Fayed, put the obvious question: *"How did Henri Paul get 20% carbon monoxide in his blood when my son had none?"*[xxv]

The obvious question is how you can get that much $CO_2$ into someone's blood stream when, due to an instantaneous death, there was no breathing, and the engine had stopped immediately.

During his last month Henri Paul had come to know what it was like to assume the Security Chief's responsibilities while the Ritz Hotel interviewed. He must have been concerned another hire may not be as accommodating as his previous colleague/boss had been. After setting up the security operation, and with a decade of service, Henri Paul now faced the possibility of being forced out by a new supervisor. Clearly, Ritz management was not taking care of Paul as a career professional.[6]

Another component of the Henri Paul enigma concerned the fact that most nations have an Embassy in Paris and many dignitaries and diplomats stay at the Ritz. Stories started to appear that Paul was in the employ of various "foreign and domestic" intelligence services. Then it was discovered he had one million francs

---

[6] The Hotel Ritz subsequently hired a former Scotland Yard Chief Superintendent John MacNamara. His background in criminal intelligence management and investigations was substantially different than Paul's Air Force Reserve security credentials.

# Session Sketch

This drawing provides a rare glimpse intelligence level RV artwork. For this exercise, people and not the building were targeted. But, this sketch could be the third floor at the North Korean Embassy in Moscow, Russia, or any building, anywhere, anytime now or for a future tasking. As a person was the target, the Hotel Ritz Paris first floor was roughed out at approximately midnight on August 31, 1997. Points of interest are:

**1)** At the top of the page, the words **Big Bldg** appear;

**2)** The various circles with an **X** inside indicates where people were standing at approximately 12:15 a.m. on August 31, 1997.

**3)** On the left, the **Main Door** is shown with an **X** representing the Door attendant. As the hall extends to the right, the various rooms are notated.

**4)** Toward the bottom is a **Business** area. As you walk from the front door, **"There is an area off to the right of this corridor which has a lot of dark paneling and dark colors with a long bar or type of counter."**

**5)** At the top is an **Alcove** with two people inside. These individual's backgrounds – conversations – futures – mental states - deaths can be targeted at any time in the future.

**6)** Where the hallway comes to a junction there is a **Man**. This is Henri Paul as he monitors the activities in both corridors. What were Paul's private thoughts? **"I associate him with a car which is parked outside and he is thinking about this car, or it seems to occupy his thoughts for some reason."**

**7)** Behind Henri Paul is the **Laborer Area**. Next to this is the drawing date and time documenting who was where when.

**8)** The hallway to the **Side Door**, **"...intersects with some kind of a smaller staff or receiving area; perhaps a back door to the building. It is recessed and that is where his car is parked."** That recessed area is shown.

**9)** McMoneagle also shows the **Formal Black Limo**'s position by the back door and correctly identified the automobile's color and manufacturer's hood ornament (bottom right).

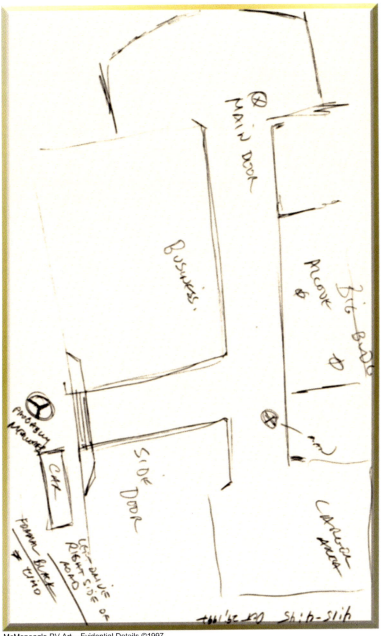

Hotel Ritz Paris first floor sketch with car (lower right) as viewed from Virginia.

(US$200,000–$250,000/$329,827-$412,285/2020) spread among eighteen bank accounts in an attempt to disguise the fact. Al-Fayed would later make the claim Paul had spent at least three years working for British intelligence. Where he got this information, or if it is true, is unknown. Paul was also allegedly in contact with the Direction General de la Securite Exterieure [DGSE] - French Intelligence. He probably worked for any number of paying interests or intelligence agencies on a spot basis.

So, we were left with a feigned alcoholic dead man; with employment and big money surveillance concerns; ordered to violate multiple traffic laws; by a romantically aggravated boss in love with the world's foremost attractive woman.

Henri Paul was uncertain about his future. He had to have been anxious about protecting his access to the Hotel Ritz time and date stamped video-monitoring system. He must have been concerned about his ability to generate big income by documenting high profile personalities, celebrities, or foreign dignitaries' arrivals and departures with anyone.

But all of a sudden, that night there was a positive side to the whole discordant affair. A rare opportunity to make a positive impression on the owner's son was at hand. In the wee hours of August 31, 1997, it would have been impossible for any driver to presume to caution a provoked Dodi Al-Fayed about safe driving on nearly deserted streets. As characterized by French Union Official Claude Luc:

> "If one of the Fayeds gives you an order,
> you follow it. No questions asked."[xxvi]

Whatever his prospects, Security Chief Henri Paul was illegally behind the wheel again. He was laid to rest in Lorient, France on September 20, 1997. Father Léon Théraud gave the sermon at Sainte Therese Church.

\* \* \*

On Saturday night, now Sunday morning August 31, a physically aggressive horde of stalkarazzi and other onlookers, estimated at approximately 130 people, jockeyed for position at the Hotel Ritz front turnstile. Diana Frances Spencer and her boyfriend Dodi, son of Egyptian born multi-millionaire Mohammad Al-Fayed, needed a second car to exit the hotel's back entrance. Because of the paparazzi, a front door - back door scheme had been set-up for their return to Dodi's apartment. Dodi would take Diana out the back leaving his personal Range Rover in front as a decoy.

**McMoneagle – Car is parked on the right side of the road (right side driving) which would rule out England, Bahamas, Hong Kong, Japan, etc. It is night and it is dark. The time for this event is current, probably 1985 to 1997. I will try and bring that down to a shorter period later.**

**The tag on the limo is elongated, with letters and numbers--which is a European style of tag** (License 688 LTV 75). **My sense is that there may actually be two colors of tags on this car, or that it has inter-changeable tags, which are changed, dependent upon where it is being operated. One is yellow with black lettering; the other is white with black lettering. It may be that there are two different colored tags on the car simultaneously—one color on one end, one color on the other.**

This is a superb surveillance example. The yellow license with black lettering was on the rear bumper. As it turned out, the color license designated a private car. The white tag is a "for hire" vehicle. From this the reader can gather the type of information available through remote viewing should this car have been driving a foreign dignitary.[7]

After some hallway discussion, Ritz chauffeur's Philippe Dourneau and Jean-Francois Musa drove two decoy vehicles to the hotel's front door. The night was clear. The temperature was 77 degrees [25C]. Their engines were revved up as Dodi and Diana hurried out the back door at 12:20 a.m.

Diana's last few minutes on earth were now inexorably caught-up in the emotional web of her incensed boyfriend and his driver's employment needs. Some paparazzi across the Rue Cabman observed them as Trevor, Diana, and then Dodi came through the turnstile and got into the Mercedes. Henri Paul pulled out and the chase was on.

**McMoneagle - Believe the car is the main focus of this**

---

[7] In Foreign Relations, these plates could indicate a restricted territory vehicle. If unauthorized, remote viewers could be tasked on who issued both types of plates to the same party. This inquiry would remain secret, while perhaps unmasking a corrupt government official, or a mole in the host country's bureaucracy.

target. The man [Paul] **may also be of interest.... I believe this target has to do with an accident that probably occurred either in the very late night hours or possibly very early morning hours. Traffic is very light and the streets are very quiet. Get a sense that there are few cars about, in a place which is usually crawling with cars.**

Associated Press

A back door security camera photograph, time stamped 12:19 a.m. just before they departed. It shows Henri Paul (left) conversing with Dodi and Diana with Trevor Rees-Jones' head in the background.

**The Mercedes is moving very fast, from what apparently is a northwest...direction. Have a sense that it goes over an overpass or cloverleaf kind of interchange, which then drops straight down, into a tunnel.**

The car traveled toward the Seine River's westbound express street referred to as the Cours la Reine. Then they entered the Alexander III & Invalides Tunnel Bridge. The tunnel is 330 meters (361 yards) long.

**McMoneagle - It [Mercedes] then exits the tunnel and covers a large curve of open road, which enters another tunnel like area, only this second tunnel is not enclosed completely. Have a sense of concrete tiers on one side... Vehicle is moving very quickly, perhaps in the neighborhood of approximately 100 MPH** [162 km/h], **maybe even a bit faster (in some spurts or straightaways).**

The curve in the road is 480 meters [.3 miles] in front of

the next tunnel, which provides an acceleration area. But with a subsequent curve and dip, it was not possible to negotiate that section of highway at high speed.

**McMoneagle - In my opinion, the driver was driving way beyond the speeds that would have been comfortable for the place and time. I believe he was well trained as a driver but not for the place or speed at which he was driving. I have a sense the driver was doing his damnedest to carry out the instructions of those he was carrying, but was operating at speeds and conditions that even he was never really trained to drive within. I think he was the professional here and was being egged on by the passengers.**

McMoneagle was correct on this detail. Paul had attended special driving courses in Stuttgart, Germany from 1988 through 1993, receiving high marks, and Dodi knew this.

These sessions took place approximately ninety days before the release of the official fifty-two page report entitled, *Accident de Passage Souterrain de l'Alma. Paris Dimanche 31 Aout 1997, Oh25. Propostition d'Analyse Scientific et Technique. Synthese et Conclusions.* French Engineer Jean Pietri had been commissioned to write an engineering crash analysis, which went on to verify this earlier remote viewing material.

The distance from the first tunnel to the Pont de l'Alma tunnel is 1.2 kilometers (.75 mile). The speed limit is 30 mph (48km). It is here that published accounts differ. Apparently, three people witnessed four to six paparazzi motorcycles attempting to pull alongside the speeding Mercedes. Other accounts say the paparazzi were a quarter of a mile behind when the Mercedes entered the tunnel. In either event, it was all futile. Notified by telephone, reporters had already assembled at Dodi's apartment entrance, million-dollar picture in mind.

**McMoneagle – The Mercedes pulls out to pass a slower moving vehicle at a point in the road where the road ahead rises upward to a secondary overpass. Because of the rise in the road, the driver can't see on-coming traffic in time to avoid it, specifically at this speed.**

The final report verified this was correct. French accident investigator Jean Pietri subsequently stated:

"*To our surprise, we observed that the field of view is extremely limited. Passing cars disappear from sight well before they actually enter the tunnel because the descending road is obscured by a retaining wall. To the left the field of vision is blocked by a row of trees.*"[xxvii]

About 40 meters (44 yards) in front of the tunnel the Mercedes hit a gap in the pavement, which further destabilized control. As the car passed a white Fiat Uno at break neck speed Henri Paul saw another car dead ahead.

**McMoneagle – I believe he sees an <u>on-coming</u> car which appears to be some kind of a black or dark green sedan. I want to say Citreon, but I'm really not sure. Probably a smaller two door car, two passengers; get a sense of dark green or green-black combination, which could mean a green a smaller two door car, two passengers; get a sense of dark green or green-black combination, which could mean a green (body) and black** (trim). [8]

Mohammad Medjahdi was driving a Citroen BX with his girlfriend Souad in the tunnel ahead of the Fiat Uno.

**McMoneagle – Dodi's last words - Have a fleeting sense that he [Paul] is being ordered to go faster and to do more erratic things, to avoid something. He (Paul) is essentially being ordered to do what he is doing.**

To avoid the **<u>on-coming</u> traffic, the Mercedes driver swerves hard to the right and catches the small car he is passing** [Fiat Uno] **with his rear bumper. Car that was passed was hit. As a result, the Mercedes slews around left, just misses the <u>on-coming</u> car, which** [it] **has just passed, and the driver then begins to over-correct his steering.**

Months after these sessions, French engineers confirmed the Mercedes did nick the Fiat Uno and over corrected to the right. Some tail light/head light debris was found. Engineers estimated that if the Mercedes was going 100 miles per hour the debris would have rolled sixteen meters (52.5 feet). That hit took place outside the tunnel and it is here the 18.9m (62ft) tire skid mark begins.[9]

---

[8] Here McMoneagle was inside looking through the Mercedes windshield. His use of *"oncoming"* describes the overtaking of cars. It does not refer to opposite direction traffic flow.

[9] The tail light pieces found in the tunnel belonged to a Fiat Uno manufactured between May 1983, and September 1989 by Seima Italiana. The white paint chips were called Bianco Corfu. When found, the car had been repainted.

**McMoneagle - The Mercedes hits the side to left slews across and hits the right, then swings back to the left, where it catches what appears to be a concrete tier or pier** (#13 pillar) **of some kind, concrete pilasters, or some kind of upright** (steel reinforced) **concrete dividers, which it hits nearly head on.**

A view of their route along the Seine River. The red arrow
(top right corner) points the direct route to Fayed's apartment.

At 12:24 am. there was an explosion sound in the tunnel. The subsequent engineering report confirmed Henri Paul's last evasive actions were viewed correctly. Various eyewitnesses recounted the collision. "Gaelle L., 40, a production assistant stated:

*"At that moment, in the opposite lane, we saw a large car approaching at high speed. This car swerved to the left, then went back to the right and crashed into the wall with its horn blaring. I should note that in front of this car, there was another, smaller car."*[xxviii]

**McMoneagle - The Mercedes apparently nearly goes end over end rear to front, but doesn't quite make it** [over the top], **instead spinning twice and winds up pointing back in the direction it was coming from.**

The car spinning $1^{1/2}$ times remains unconfirmed. However, there was enough inertia for the car to have spun 540 degrees when the rear wheels were off the ground. The impact was so hard that the forward roof area was crushed down to the level of the driver's knees. This is further substantiated by the fact Diana was found facing backward in the back seat, which would not have happened with a simple 180-degree turn. N*ewsweek Magazine* reported French police estimated the car had slowed down to 85 mph at the point of impact.[xxix]

The entire trip had taken about four minutes. Trevor Rees-

Jones did not leave the hospital until October 4 - thirty-four days later. He could only recall the Fiat Uno.

**Rees-Jones**: *"It seems to me there was one white car with a boot which opened at the back* [hatch back]*, and three doors but I don't remember anything else."*ˣˣˣ

Aware Henri Paul did not have alcohol in his system, we sought clarification to research about drugs in his blood stream.

**McMoneagle - Substance review - I believe if the driver had drugs in his system, whatever kind they were, they were not there by his own hand. I have this sort of strange feeling that he was not deliberately drugged to hurt anyone, but maybe he was drugged to get the car stopped along the route for the "photographers" to get their shots. In other words, his control was tampered with by outside influences. I don't think he was drunk, possibly drugged, but not drunk.**

Here the research came full circle. The paparazzi had attempted to slow the Hotel Ritz airport shuttle vehicles earlier that afternoon on the drive from the airport. Once it was discovered, Henri Paul had been an informant for domestic as well as foreign intelligence services we went back to McMoneagle. Could the British government have been involved?

**McMoneagle - My sense is that MI-5** (British Intelligence) **did not put the stuff in his drink. However, one might contemplate that if he** [Paul] **was willing to take money from foreign intelligence operatives, he most certainly would have been open to taking money from the Paparazzi. Maybe they were hedging their bets by having a small "drink" with him in the bar before he started driving.**

And what of the high carbon dioxide levels in Dodi's blood stream? Since this viewing, there were reports of a carbon monoxide suicide in Paris that night.

**McMoneagle - You have to open your perception a little bit here. He did not have to have any evidence of $CO_2$ in his blood for them to find $CO_2$ in a blood sample. You only have to switch the samples at the hospital, the morgue, or the lab. Or, pay off the guy who is doing the tests. You could also conceivably rig the test equipment. Also, there are drugs, which will give a false reading as well.**

**His being drugged enough to cause the accident could**

be attributed to a drug delivered in coffee, tea, or a drink beforehand. It could also have been sprayed on the inner edge of his door handle (driver's side), painted on the steering wheel, or inside a pair of driving gloves. He could have been shot with a needle delivery system, or pricked his hand, finger, leg, or almost any part of his anatomy on a delivery system getting into or out of the car. It can even be filmed across the pages of a book or map that he might have used to check directions on.

If he had a normal medical condition, they could have used a drug, which reacts violently with the drugs he is already taking for the medical condition. In which case they would either get false readings, or evidence of his medicinal drug, plus some other known drug which would not have been viewed as culprit in the event, simply because no one recognized the possible expected reaction. You also have problems with drugs which are binary in nature and can be delivered in two sittings, so to speak, where the victim gets part A in the morning with breakfast, part B in the evening with dinner, both of which are enzymes and when mixed... cause everything from hallucinogenic behavior, to strokes.

Now we turned to what Dodi and Diana where thinking.

**McMoneagle - Back seat travelers - MAJOR PROBLEM:** When I try to access others who might have been in the car, I get heavy [analytic] overlay and interference as relates to Diana's death in France. My head fills up with all kinds of motorcycles, and all kinds of news... that was being broadcast about the incident. I believe there were at least two others in this target car, but digging anything out of the overlay is completely impossible.

There is a sense from the people in the back seat that they want to be alone together, but again, I then get overwhelmed with all the Princess Diana stuff... and it all runs together. So, I can't begin to tell where [the] overlay begins and real data ends. Would prefer to say nothing.

It's rather interesting. I actually have not opened the envelope nor have a clue as to the real target here; but I am being overwhelmed with overlay which is self generated. Must have been a lot of energy around the Princess Diana stuff. Better to just go no further with it. End of Session.

An abrupt stop, on a then well-known topic, due to analytic overlay. This is a graphic demonstration of the differences between military remote viewers, storefront psychics or hot lines. The media had been saturated with Princess Diana coverage in the period between the accident and this tasking. A psychic hot-liner would have been able to talk and bill without end about what they "saw." One Operation Star Gate military remote viewer commented, "There are many "*psychics*" who have taken this type of gibberish to a finely honed skill."[xxxi] But, when McMoneagle got to the Mercedes back seat, he stopped the session. In intelligence work when you are not sure of your viewing, you must say so. Any elaboration is unethical as in life and death situations, military viewers must stay grounded in the target's realities.

Analytic Overlay [AOL] is terminology within the Controlled Remote Viewing [CRV] protocols developed by Mr. Ingo Swann for the U.S. Military Intelligence Community at the Stanford Research Institute as they developed the nomenclature. AOL can generate bad data. So, can anything be done about it?

McMoneagle - Military research - There were a number of experiments which were run to examine whether or not a remote viewer can identify "AOL" while in session. We found that it could be rarely demonstrated. Most viewers are unable to tell (accurately or consistently) when something was AOL or when it wasn't, while in session.

Facts are; Evidence produced within labs suggests that no one methodology is capable of identifying and extinguishing AOL any better than another over the long haul.

There have been significant runs of very low AOL or displays of almost no AOL which have been done by individual remote viewers. So, there are indications that some people might have a talent for producing less AOL than others. But it does not appear to be method driven since it doesn't hold up in testing across all remote viewers using the same method.

So, why should identifying AOL be important??? It is important because, while you are attempting to learn remote viewing (regardless of method), it makes you think about how and why you are "thinking" about something. It is meant to reduce the speed by which you automatically jump to a conclusion. It also supports the structure and keeps one

**within it (at least until one becomes proficient enough to no longer need it.)**

After the impact, eyewitnesses saw a motorcycle 30 to 40 meters behind the Mercedes slow down to observe the accident and then accelerate away from the scene. At 12:26 a.m., the Paris Fire Department - Sapeurs-Pompiers Unit - received a cell phone call from a Gaelle who was in the tunnel. Within one minute another call went out to the "service d'aid medicale urgente" (SAMU) - a civilian emergency medical service.

Inside the wreck, Diana and bodyguard Trevor Rees-Jones were still alive. One eyewitness said he heard a woman crying loudly. One of the paparazzi, Romuald Rat, indicated Diana was conscious. He claimed he told her to stay calm; that help was on the way.

# Aftermath

Now pandemonium broke out as the Press fought each other to get the new million dollar shot. One photographer leaned into the car to reposition Dodi's corpse for a posed picture. Someone else came with video equipment. Within five minutes, Police Officers Lion Gagliardone and Sebastien Dorzee plowed through the crowd to the car. The police report stated:

"*I observe the occupants in the vehicle are in a very grave state. I immediately repeat the call for aid and request police reinforcements, being un-able to contain the photographers….*"[xxxii]

Officer Dorzee: "*I finally got to the vehicle... The rear passenger* (Diana) *was also alive... She seemed to be in better shape* (than Rees-Jones). *However, blood flowed from her mouth and nose. There was a deep gash on her forehead. She murmured in English, but I didn't understand what she said. Perhaps 'My God!'*"[xxxiii]

Ultimately, six paparazzi were held in connection with the frenzy in the tunnel. They were arrested on suspicion of involuntary homicide and failure to assist persons in danger. Excepting the 24-year-old Romuald Rat, 40 was the average age of those arrested. Twenty film rolls were confiscated providing police with the photographic evidence they needed to confirm each man's activities that night. Three paparazzi got away.

There are no Miranda rights in France, nor is there a right to call an attorney. French authorities can hold a suspect for forty-eight hours before the prisoner must be formally charged or set free. However, it is certain Henri Paul did not have to be drunk or drugged to have had an accident at that speed.

The former Princess of Wales, Diana Spencer, arrived at the Hospital de la Pitie-Salpetriere at 2:00 a.m. She was pronounced dead at 4:00 a.m. It was then she attempted to contact her son William in Scotland. "William had had a difficult night sleep and had woken many times. That morning he had known, he said, that something awful was going to happen."xxxiv When he was told of his mother's death he said, "*I knew something was wrong. I kept waking up all night.*"xxxv

At 5:00 p.m. Prince Charles, 48, flew into Villacoublay military airfield outside Paris from Aberdeen, Scotland with Diana's sisters Sarah McCorquodale and Jane Fellows. "Diana's sisters spent most of the flight to Paris in tears. The Prince was controlled but clearly very shaken."xxxvi By 5:40 p.m., he was greeted at the hospital by the French President and Mrs. Jacque Chirac (1995-2007). Charles was led into a room with his two ex-sisters-in-laws where Diana lay in a coffin. He asked to be alone with the body for a moment. When he came out his eyes were red. The accident was 368 days after the finalization of their divorce.

Diana's coffin, draped in the Royal Standard's yellow and maroon, was flown home by an honor guard in a British Royal Air Force BAe146 aircraft to Northolt Air Force Base in England. She was then taken to the Chapel Royal at Saint James Place.

Undertaken by Levertons, her September 6 funeral was the largest in England since the death of former Prime Minister and Nobel Literature Prize winner Winston Churchill [1874-1965]. After the morning funeral, it was reported a million people lined the route as the body was taken from London's Westminster Abby. Different accounts estimated two to three billion people watched the day's events as the car traveled the seventy-five miles to Althorpe House. Late that afternoon her body was laid to rest on a 1,254 sq. meter (13,500 sqft) island called The Oval in a lake on the Spencer's ancestral grounds. The four hundred-year-old estate was then partially turned into a tourist attraction.

On September 9, 1997, the week after Diana was buried

the Al-Fayed attorney filed civil law suits against the French periodicals *France-Dimanche* and *Paris-Match*. The complaint specified invasion of privacy with willful and wanton reckless endangerment when helicoptering "stalkerazzi" got too close over the Fayed's villa in St. Tropez. But, for the Hotel Ritz, the question became who bears responsibility for the accident? Before 1997 was out, the Fayed, Spencer, Rees-Jones and Paul families had all filed papers to be made civil parties to the investigation. Under French law, this allows them to investigate the case file and participate in any damage awards. And as for the Paparazzi's fate:

*"In accordance with articles 175, 176 and 177 of the Code of Penal Procedure; The examining magistrates find that there is no case to answer in the case of the state versus the above named* [Photographers].*"*[xxxvii] (Case Dismissed)

In July of 2004, after the planning, funding and construction were completed, Queen Elizabeth II personally opened the Princess of Wales Memorial Fountain in the southwest corner of London's fashionable Hyde Park.

Then, in April 2008, after a three year investigation costing $7.3 million ($12 million+/2020), a six month long British report was released which included the testimony of 278 witnesses with more than 600 exhibits generating an 832 page report stating:

*"Our conclusion is that, on the evidence available at this time, there was no conspiracy to murder any of the occupants of the car,"* Lord Stevens of Kirkwhelpington, who led the inquiry, told reporters as he presented his findings here. *"This was a tragic accident."*[xxxviii]

In September of 2012, the French magazine *Closer* published paparazzi photos of Diana's eldest son's wife Kate Middleton sunbathing topless while at the Queen's nephew, Lord Linley's French chateau. A publically released statement on behalf of the Duke and Duchess said:

*"The incident is reminiscent of the worst excesses of the press and paparazzi during the life of Diana, Princess of Wales, and all the more upsetting to The Duke and Duchess for being so."*

And as for the need to use remote viewing protocols:

**McMoneagle - Pick whatever method you intend to pursue and stick to it like glue. AOL** (Analytic Overlay) **is a fact of life and this will always be so.** Those of you who can eventually see your way to controlling your inner-driven or more personalized prejudice while internally processing, will probably improve somewhat in reducing AOLs, but AOLs will never entirely go away.

**CRV** (Controlled Remote Viewing) is a "method" derived from a method the military used while attempting to "train" people to understand both protocol as well as what is going on in a remote viewer's head (such as processing or the lack thereof).

I would add that formal testing in the SRI Lab showed that regardless of technique or methodology utilized, most viewers were unable to consistently identify AOLs when asked to identify them prior to feedback. I have to say most, because "a couple viewers" were able to do so during significant runs--but this is inherently talent based and not the general or common rule. I remind you all of what is termed the "AH-HA". If it were not for the Ah-ha's, there would not have been a program. At the end of the road, almost anything is right when you have finally come to understand that it is an inherent part of our nature and then you just simply can do it.

-----------

*The worst term of all is "psychic." No stable definition has ever been established for it, and there are great hazards in attempting to utilize a term which has not much in the way of an agreed-upon definition.*

*Supporters do assume that it refers to extraordinary, non-normal (paranormal) activities of mind. But skeptics assume it refers to illusion, derangement and a variety of non-normal or abnormal clinical psychopathologies."*

Remote Viewing - One of the Superpowers of the Human Bio-Mind; Remote Viewing and its Conceptual Nomenclature Problems by Ingo Swann (09Jan96)

# Part II

What you are about to read is the data the Intelligence Community would have received had they tasked this event in the interest of the People of the United States of America.

# Interview Clarification

Question: Generally speaking, how much...information should be given a viewer in operations / applications?

**Joseph McMoneagle**: None. Zero. What you can do if the target requires a response or a description of an individual, you can say, "*Describe the individual at* (whatever location)" and the location needs to be hidden (would be a number, for instance). If you were targeting let's say a church, and there was an individual in that church, the church would be coded as say, "location A1". It would then say, "*describe individual at location A1*".

Under no condition can you give any information that is directly pertinent to the target. There is never any front-loading. The reason for this is because the entire concept of remote viewing is that an individual is forced, has no choice, but to use their psi ability to answer the requirement. Any info that is given in any way, or form, modifies that response in a way that removes / reduces the probability of accuracy.

----------

"Detachment G's[10] viewers looked at projects ranging from the status of a cement plant in a hostile country to the location of Soviet troops in Cuba. Important North Korean personalities were targeted, as well as underground facilities in Europe, chemical weapons in Afghanistan, the presence of electronic bugs in the new U.S. embassy in Moscow, the activities of a KGB general officer, a missing U.S. helicopter, tunnels under the Korean Demilitarized Zone, and numerous buildings whose purposes were unknown to U.S. Intelligence."

Paul H. Smith – Operation Star Gate Remote Viewer
In *Reading the Enemy's Mind*

---

[10] Det G [Detachment G] was the remote viewing program's code name as it evolved from Operation 'Gondola Wish' to Operation 'Grill Flame'. These were the viewers to make the Army's cut between December 1978 and January 1979. "The Army Chief of Staff for Intelligence, Major General Thompson, officially decreed that the program name, embodied in Det G, would be the focal point for all Army involvement in parapsychology and remote viewing." Op cit. Smith

Amelia Earhart

# The Last Flight
*of*

# Amelia

# Earhart

Including a
# Crash Site Map

Surface navigation is known, to
the profession, as an inexact science.
Navigator Fred Noonan

*Each time we make a choice, we pay.*
Excerpted from her poem *Courage*

The cryptic report went in two directions. From U.S. Coast Guard Cutter Itasca's radioman Leo G. Bellarts to U.S. Twelfth District Naval Headquarters, Hawaii and to Coast Guard Headquarters in San Francisco, California:

*Earhart contact 0742 (7:42 am) reported one half hour fuel and no land fall. Position doubtful. (Previous) Contact (at) 0646 reported one hundred miles from Itasca but no relative bearing. (Her message) ...at 0843 reported line of position 157 dash 337 but no reference point. Presume Howland (Island). Estimate 1200 (noon) for maximum time aloft and if non-arrival by that time will commence search Northwest quadrant from Howland as most probable area. Understand she will float for limited time.*[xxxix]

United States Coast Guard Cutter *Itasca*'s Radioman Leo G. Bellarts

The "Queen of the Sky" was in trouble. Born thirty minutes before midnight on July 24, 1897 on N. Terrace Street in Atchison, Kansas, Amelia Mary Earhart had made International news by being the first woman to passenger across the Atlantic Ocean on June 17-18, 1928 in a Fokker F VIII seaplane. This was less than 25 years after inventors Orville and Wilbur Wright had first flown at Kitty Hawk, North Carolina on December 17, 1903. Based on that technology, her trip was considered dangerous.

This flight was just thirteen months after Charles A. Lindbergh (1902-1974) stunned the world by flying non-stop New York to Paris on May 20-21, 1927. And though many Trans-Atlantic flights had taken place since, Amelia became the second individual in history to solo over the Atlantic Ocean flying New-foundland to Culmore near Londonderry, Northern Ireland on Lindbergh's fifth anniversary. She had flown 2,026 miles (3,261 km) in 15 hours, 18 minutes. With this, she captured the public's imagination and provided the perfect diversion from the general misery of a population caught up in the nation's worst depression.

Amelia enjoyed flying and continued her record setting exploits. Now she was involved in her longest and most prestigious flight yet. She would circumnavigate the globe as close to the equator as possible. She stated:

*I have a feeling*, she said, *that there is just one more good flight left in my system, and I hope this is it. Anyway, when I finish this job, I mean to give up major long distance flights.*[xl]

In support of this effort, Indiana's Purdue University loaned her the most advanced aircraft of the day – the Lockheed Electra 10E.

Amelia was fifteen when the *Titanic* sank. She was twenty during the Russian Revolution. Though her life and times are known, the great mystery has always been what became of the thirty-nine year old pilot? How did she simply vanish? This mystery presented a remote viewing challenge in that no targeting co-ordinates existed. To compensate we observed her plane at the Lae City Airfield in Papua, New Guinea and used a remote viewing technique known as entropy to bring the viewer to the crash site. Now Joseph McMoneagle looked at a double blind envelope on the table in the foothills of the Blue Ridge Mountains in Virginia.

**McMoneagle – (Target) ...seems to center around some kind of an island, or a mountain (spine) jutting up out of water. So far, looks like some kind of an accident involving water... Seems to be some confusion around communicating as well.**

Everything was set. By way of her contacts with America's First Lady, Eleanor Roosevelt (1884-1962), the United States Government had the *USS Ontario* patrolling half way between the origin Lae City Airport and Howland Island to help guide Amelia across the Pacific Ocean. A Chelan class U.S. Coast Guard Cutter *Itasca* was also positioned northwest of Howland to serve as a homing vessel. The 250-foot, 1,979 ton, 3,220 horsepower vessel had a 16 knot top speed with which to conduct a rescue.[xli]

Amelia's husband, George Palmer Putnam owned Putnam Publishing, Inc. They worked out all the logistics with the Pratt & Whitney and Standard Oil Companies. The former was to make spare parts available on the route. The latter was to maintain avia-tion fuel stocks at those airfields. The U.S. Government worked out the temporary visas and landing rights in the various countries.

Friends: Amelia Earhart, 37, with First Lady Eleanor Roosevelt, 51, at the March 2, 1935 National Geographic Society luncheon honoring Amelia.

On June 1, 1937 Amelia Earhart, and her navigator Fred Noonan, departed Miami, Florida for San Juan, Puerto Rico. At the airport, "A great crowd was gathering. At four minutes past six AE closed and fastened the hatch. Ground attendants signaled 'All clear'. The pilot's slim fingers flashed against the cockpit window, the motors revved up, the chocks were pulled out, the wheels began to turn, and thirty seconds later, the ship was in the air. From the roof of the Administration Building, standing with my son David, I watched the silver Electra rise and wheel around and disappear southeast into the morning."[xlii] So wrote George Palmer Putnam. He would never see his wife again.

From San Juan, Puerto Rico, the flight went to Venezuela and Brazil where they crossed the Atlantic Ocean to Africa. This African leg was seven stops across the continent from modern Dakar, Senegal over to Assab, Ethiopia with a stop at Khartoum. From there they flew on to Karachi, Pakistan, Calcutta, India, Rangoon, Burma (Myanmar since 1989), to Bangkok, Thailand and on to Singapore. From there it was over Indonesia to Darwin, Australia, then northeast up to Lae City in Papua, New Guinea.

Now, one month and almost twenty thousand miles later, the long and eventful journey was nearing its end. Amelia had only three segments and 7,000 miles to go across the Pacific Ocean to get to the States. The next segment was from Lae City Airport to Howland Island. These 2,556 miles (4,113km) would take her approximately half way to the Hawaiian Islands.

This type of water down aircraft targeting had precedence in U.S. military history. In March, 1979, a reconnaissance configured Soviet Tupolev-22 bomber crashed somewhere in the nation of Zaire. The aircraft, code named "Blinder" by NATO, went down somewhere deep in the jungle and had radioed no final position.

Due to a remote viewing performed at Wright Patterson Air Force Base, the Americans were able to beat the Russians to their plane. President Carter (1977-1981) was aware of the Remote Viewing program at the Stanford Research Institute and had no objections to this methodology. The former President later recounted the affair to a college student group. "By the end of the Carter Administration the SRI program was reaching its peak. Operational targets flowed in, remote viewing data flowed out, and operations oriented experiments continued."[xliii]

With destination unknown, our double blind Earhart envelop was merely another water target, except that the viewer was Joseph McMoneagle, Amelia is a civilian target, and the point in time is 10:00 a.m. July 1, 1937 at Lae City Airport, New Guinea.

**McMoneagle – Have a sense that I am looking down onto some kind of an island, which has very thick jungle and lots of very tall and rugged mountains along a double spine. The place I am currently situated over is approximately two thirds down the island and on what appears to be a general northern coast line in a sort of crotch like area between two ridge lines of mountains. One spine leads to the south** (Bismarck Range) **and one leads across the northern rim or edge of the island** (Northern New Guinea Range).

<u>**Lae Airfield**</u> - **I'm looking down on a dirt or primitive road, which seems to parallel a river** (Markham) **that runs into the foothills of the two converging mountain spines. There is essentially nothing here except for village huts and what appears to be a seaplane facility connected to a newly constructed dirt airfield. Well, dirt isn't exactly correct. The runway is some kind of a sand and dirt mix; very hard pack, but having a ruggedness about it. The parking area is constructed of concrete squares, approximately three by three feet, and covered with what appears to be crushed coral, shells, and about six inches thick. (I) Think this airport facility is probably good for older planes with larger wheels and light cargo.**

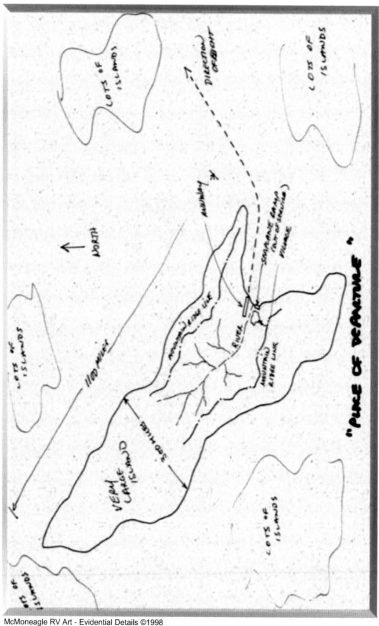

McMoneagle RV Art - Evidential Details ©1998

McMoneagle's map from **10,000 feet**. His **Place of Departure** shows New Guinea with the proper placement of the Lae City Airport on the Huon Gulf in the Solomon Sea. Above left it says, **Very Large Island**. Lower center an arrow points to a **Seaplane Ramp (out of service)**. The **Runway** and flight path are also shown. The **Lots of Islands** are the Bismarck-New Britain Archipelagos.

The runway extends in a general east to west config-uration with the wind there being almost constantly out of the west to the east or in rare cases, east to west. The runway is actually built up on one end so that it extends outward toward what appears to be a <u>sudden drop-off over water</u>. I would also add that I get a strong sense this is a very primitive runway, as it is completely enclosed with jungle. The jungle trees have been pushed back quite a way, perhaps six hundred feet from the runway. But, many of these trees are still quite high (some in excess of 100 feet tall), which makes this a very hazardous runway to land on from any direction other than coming in dead-on, or centered on either end. The seaplane facility seems to be in disrepair or is no longer used, having been replaced by this (3,000 foot) runway.

Lae City airfield was, "Built without government permission by Cecil J. Levien, on behalf of Guinea Gold N.L., to assist the gold mine...in 1927. The largest pre-war aircraft to use the airport were the Junkers G31 Tri-Motor, in service to the gold fields at Bulolo. The problem with Lae's east/west runway was that it ran directly in-to hills, limiting the size of aircraft able to land."[xliv] These airplanes operated until Japanese fighter planes destroyed three of them on January 21, 1942. The fourth was removed to Australia. After World War II, a new 5,800 foot (1768m) hard surface runway was built.

**McMoneagle – Indonesia - Going back to the island, I would say that it is unusually large for an island in this region. If one were to drift up to about 10,000 feet and look around, there are literally hundreds of smaller islands throughout the entire area as far as the eye can see.**

The aircraft at Lae City airport that morning were unknown to history. Based on his intelligence background, McMoneagle automatically looked inside each airplane to acquire the target.

**McMoneagle – There are what appear to be three planes on the ground. Two of them are larger than a third. Two of these planes are twin engine, and the third has three engines. The plane with three engines** (Junker G31) **is general-ly a passenger carrying aircraft, which is rigged out to carry a minimum of 12 people and light cargo.**

**The second larger plane is also rigged for some pas-sengers or cargo. It has what appears to be some kind of folding webbed or woven seats along both sides half way**

down the aisle, and a large double door at the rear for loading great amounts of cargo. I get a sense that the smaller plane and the larger double-side door plane are probably tail draggers, and the triple engine plane is not. It seems to sit upright more squarely with the ground and has kind of a unique tail wheel of some kind.

Courtesy James Colloquy through Ann Holtgren Pellegreno
A Lae City, New Guinea Airport (center) banking runway approach as seen by Amelia and Fred in 1937, with the Markham River (top left corner).

Here the historian can imagine Earhart's plane taxiing to the runway's furthest end (lower right side) before taking off over the edge (top left).

We were unable to identify the second aircraft, but it was probably a now defunct Guinea Airways (1930-1950) airliner.

We were able to confirm McMoneagle's statement about the Junkers G31 Tri-motor having a unique tail wheel/skid (**red circle**).

**McMoneagle – The Electra - The third plane is a twin engine, smaller, and has no room for cargo or people. It appears to have additional fuel tanks in its cargo area and so it is either used for carrying fuel from port to port, or the transfer of some other chemical besides fuel in fuel like tanks.**

The Bulolo gold field needed bulk chemicals. Pilot Bert Heath flew half hour supply trips between the Lae City Airfield and the Bulolo Gold Dredging Company's airfield. Its position is shown on McMoneagle's map notated as "village" (p. 48). A gold mining logistics system resembles a real life Operation Star Gate tasking.

Amelia had first flown the new Electra 10E on July 22, 1936 taking off from an airstrip in Burbank California. "'*It was simply elegant*,' she said to mechanics who crowded round the shining thing, with its 55 foot wing span, the two 550 hp (Pratt & Whitney) Wasp engines, (with) the cruising radius of 4,500 miles."[xlv] Her 7,000 lb. aircraft was a ten-seat passenger plane modified to haul 1100 gallons of fuel. The plane cruised at 150-160 miles per hour with a top speed of 210-215 mph (338–346kph).

**McMoneagle - I would guess the time and dates for the above to be somewhere in maybe a pre - 1950 period, because all of the planes and equipment feel appropriate to that period. The radios are cumbersome and heavy, requiring large power supplies and backup batteries. I believe the plane has electric starters, but also has a "Kauffman" (spelling may be incorrect) backup, which would date it to about a ten year plus or minus period (pre-war to post-war), circa 1930 to 1950.**

Plane also has something funny with its tail; like it isn't a normal upright or vertical fin (dual rudder). This probably has something to do with a strange flight characteristic pertinent to this particular kind of plane, perhaps a loss of control in heavy weather, or when executing specific kinds of turns; maybe a direct result of the kinds of engines, where or how they are mounted.

There is a lot of activity on the ground around the smaller of the planes and there seems to be some fuss about antennas or something like that. I get a sense that there are numbers of antennas on this plane, one of which is not very satisfactory to the pilot. Get a sense that there are at least six people present, two women (Mrs. Chater) and four men (Mr. Chater, Noonan, Jacobson and Collopy). One of the women is either the pilot or co-pilot, which seems to be quite unusual for some reason. General feeling seems to be quite a bit of reluctance about taking off. There's some argument about fuel loads and distance, as well as much concern about weather.

Both the male (Noonan) and female have gotten in and out of the plane and both have sat in essentially both seats a number of times and started engines and run them out for a few minutes while the others are checking on something outside. I get a very strong sense that the engines are being tuned in some way for variances in heat or temperature. I also get a feeling of great anticipation, as this feels like a very tropical place and there is concern about whether they should wait any longer for takeoff, since the heat is growing and it will affect the distance of run out when they attempt to lift off.

Some kind of decision is made that they should go before the sun gets much higher and the air gets any thinner. There is also some confusion about radio frequencies. The woman doesn't want to use one of the frequency sets, but the others are telling her that she has to because it has something to do with line of sight versus distance. One of the men keeps telling her that the lower the frequency the better, but she is very disagreeable about it, primarily because of the size or length of the antenna which is required. Why this should be a problem, I don't know. It may be that too many antennas in some way degrade the flying characteristics of the aircraft, or something like that.

**Looking back at the aircraft** (NR 16020), **I have to say that I get a very good feeling about it. It is a machine that has been well used, but at the same time, very well taken care of.** (Sensing the airplane is not Earharts) **Whomever this aircraft belongs to, they know it, and its faults, from top to bottom.**

Amelia in the co-pilot position. She and Noonan would have been harnessed into these seats. The historian can see how easy it was for Fred to read the gauges.

Research showed this was correct. Before flying the Atlantic Ocean, the engines had been checked and overhauled by Pan American mechanics in Fortaleza, Brazil on June 5. Again on June 15 in Karachi Pakistan, aviation mechanics from Imperial Airways and instrument specialists with the British Royal Air Force, "put the plane back into top condition."[xlvi] Then in Bandoeng, Java, in what were the Dutch East Indies, from June 21 - 27, engine and instrument calibration work took place on two occasions.

**McMoneagle - It is also a very stable flying platform, but probably a little bit too small for the type of flying it is being used for. I see absolutely nothing wrong with the aircraft, other than the fact that it is very, very heavy; which implies that it is being used for distance. Given the location, I suspect that they are trying for distance over a great deal of water given this is essentially an island.**

I don't get anything really remarkable about the events or the takeoff from this airport, other than it seems to be unique that the pilot might be female. She also seems to be clearly in charge — that is making all the decisions. Cruise altitude, wind speed, direction, fuel load, weight, aircraft, attitudes, essentially everything I can sense seems to be just fine. There may be one small problem with some form of hydraulic system under the left or port engine. It may have something to do with landing gear, but it is a minor one and is not one that anyone would be very upset about.

This appears to be new information. But, extensive aircraft repairs were made after Amelia's take off crash at Wheeler airfield in Honolulu, Hawaii, on March 20, 1937. The landing gear attachment points were re-engineered and strengthen so extensively that the Bureau of Air Commerce had to sign off on their redesign.

McMoneagle – Amelia - The woman is approximately five feet, eight inches tall. She is taller than what would be considered average, and somewhat lanky or thin looking; definitely not frail however. She is well tanned, or has somewhat of a weathered appearance, short hair, and is wearing a blouse... She also has what appears to be a leather type jacket, which she wears when it gets cold. I have a sense that she is also wearing near knee-length lined boots... Her hair is dark, probably brown, as well as her eyes. Her features are angular, her nose is somewhat pointed, and she has what appears to be a small scar on the left side of her head just below the eye line. She is probably about mid 30's (39)...

The other person in the plane was flight navigator Frederick Joseph Noonan (1893-1937). He was a tall Irishman who had spent many years on merchant ships. Raised in Cook County Illinois, he joined the English Navy as an officer aboard a munitions transport vessel. He was 22 years at sea.[xlvii]

During the late 1920's Noonan had learned to fly. He pioneered aerial direction finding and earned a living as a navigational instructor in the emerging airline industry. Hired in 1930 by Pan American World Airways (1927-2013), he was a commercial pilot, navigator, airport manager, and system wide airport inspector. He also developed Pam Am's transpacific aviation routes.

In November, 1935 he had served as navigator when the large four engine *China Clipper* opened the Pacific Trade Routes from the United States.[xlviii] As a flight navigation author, he was introduced to Amelia Earhart and George Putnam as one of the world's best. But Putnam raised questions about his suitability because Noonan was rumored to be a heavy drinker. This was evident enough that, in spite of his major contributions and versatility, Pan American Airlines let him go in early 1937.

Amelia in charge as she spoke to navigator Fred Noonan, 44, on June 28, 1937 in Darwin, Australia.

**McMoneagle – Fred Noonan - The man is apparently tall but thin. I would consider him to be lanky as well. He is apparently there as both a navigator as well as a backup pilot. Or at least he is sitting in that seat. He has sunken features and his skin is dark. He also has a deep voice, but is a soft-**

spoken individual as well. He is about six feet to six feet and one inch in height, about 145 to 150 pounds; very strong, for his age, which is about 45 years old, perhaps a shade younger. His hair is either black or dark brown, and is just beginning to show some silver. Probably from how seriously he takes his job.

I think these two are good friends and get along fairly well together. I sense no animosities between them, no arguments seem to exist, nor disagreements of any significance. They appear to work very well together. Can see absolutely no problem with their flight or plane on the specific target day.

That March, Noonan had married Mary B. Martinelli in Yuma, Arizona. One wonders if she would have allowed her groom to fly with Amelia if she had been aware of her ongoing death premonitions. They were so cogent Amelia wrote and verbalized them repeatedly over the years.

In what has gone largely undocumented, one day out of the blue, Amelia said to her husband George, *"...as one who may be imagining or simply comprehending a fact*, she said slowly, '*I think probably, GP that I'll not live--to be old.'"*[xlix] She also took the time to write goodbye death premonition letters before specific flights. Of three that survive, one was written nine years earlier dated May 20, 1928:

*Dearest Dad:*

*Hooray for the last grand adventure! I wish I had won, but it was worthwhile anyway. You know that I have no faith we'll meet anywhere again, but I wish we might. Anyway, good-bye and good luck to you. Affectionately, your doter, Mill.*

At another time, Amelia wrote her mother:

*Even though I have lost, the adventure was worthwhile. Our family tends to be too secure. My life has really been very happy, and I don't mind contemplating its end in the midst of it.*[l]

And to her sister:

*I have tried to play for a large stake, and if I succeed all will be well. If I don't I shall be happy to pop off in the midst of such an adventure.*[li]

In less than two months of married life, Mary Noonan said her last farewell when Fred went to meet-up with Amelia on May 20 for their around the world flight. Unemployed, he needed to make money to put their marriage on a better financial footing. One can imagine how Mary might have cautioned Fred if she had known Amelia told her husband George: "Amelia often said to me, *'When I go, I'd like best to go in my plane. Quickly.'*"[lii]

**McMoneagle – Weather at takeoff is clear, scudding clouds, generally flowing from a east-northeast to west-south-west direction at about 10 to 15 knots; what one would have to call a sharp ocean breeze.**

A decision was made to go before the air got any thinner.

**McMoneagle – Two people onboard. Woman is sitting in the left-hand seat, and a man is sitting in the right hand seat. Both seats are flush back against a bulkhead or metallic wall. There is a center console, and apparently extra radio or backup radio equipment. There is also some kind of a device in the central section of roof, which appears to have some significance to them, which I do not think is normally associated with this aircraft. A surveillance device perhaps, but does not actually quite fit that definition. It rotates.**

This was the plane's high frequency loop antenna. This is when McMoneagle would have determined if Earhart was a spy.

After their departure a telegram was received by the *Press Tribune* in Oakland, California stamped local time 3:04 a.m., July 2. It read in part:

*Lockheed stands ready for longest hop weighted with gasoline and oil to capacity however clouds and <u>wind blowing wrong way</u>. Considered keeping her on ground today. In addition FN* (Fred Noonan) *has been unable account <u>radio difficulties</u> to set his chronometers; lack knowledge* (of) *their fastness or slowness.*[liii]

**McMoneagle - Takeoff – It feels like mid-morning, (10:00 a.m.) temperature is already about 90 degrees (32C) and climbing. Get a strong sense the aircraft uses every bit of runway getting off the ground, perhaps even <u>dropping</u> a bit as it leaves the drop-off at the end over the water. Do not get a sense that the airplane is climbing very rapidly however. It seems to stay quite low as it curves slightly to the north of due east and leaves the area.**

Amelia Earhart with Lockheed's Clarence Williams. The picture shows how closely the pilot and navigator worked together.

Research confirmed this was correct. The runway did allow for a drop of approximately 25 feet to the ocean. Commercial pilot Bert Heath was in a holding pattern waiting to land at the airport. He reported the plane went, "'*over the drop-off,*' flying so low over the sea that the propellers were '*throwing spray.*'"[liv] Lae City Airport's District Superintendent for Civil Aviation, James A. Collopy, reported:

*When it did leave it sank away but by this time over the sea. It continued to sink* (to) *about five or six feet above the water and had not climbed to more than 100 feet before it disappeared from sight.*[lv]

Not lifting more than 100 feet before they were out of sight is cautious. Also during takeoff, Mr. McMoneagle viewed a problem we were unable to corroborate for many years.

**McMoneagle – There's some kind of a broken part on the plane, which was either broken at take-off, or broken a lot earlier that has some effect on all this as well; maybe an antenna connection. These planes were notorious for needing multiple "cut antenna" systems, and always having trouble with one antenna or another going out all the time.**

Earhart's Lae City take off shows a puff of smoke from what is likely the plane's rear belly antenna mast dragging the ground, thereby supplying an Evidential Detail.

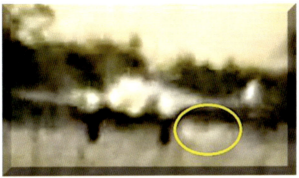

A close up of the dust (yellow circle) as the aft belly antenna mast was likely dragging the airfield before it broke off, assuring communications problems.

Jeff Glickman, of Phototek, Inc. is a Board Certified Forensic Examiner, and a Fellow at the American College of Forensic Examiners, He confirmed the belly antenna mast had broken away after the plane started down the runway. This was important enough for McMoneagle to mention twice.

**McMoneagle – August, 1998 - The plane also lost something after takeoff, so it might have lost a piece or segment of a control surface or something that was significant. Can't tell what it is, (it) doesn't seem to have any specific shape or form, but I do get a sense that it directly contributed in some way to the eventual crash.**

Until Mr. Glickman's efforts, we had had no way to confirm this detail. In what fell right into our lap, McMoneagle appeared to have been the first to put in writing the loss of an "*antenna connection*" and the Phototek, Inc. forensic analyst confirmed it.

"As the machine was leaving the ground, the following report was received at the airport wireless station. It read in part:

*Accurate forecast difficult account lack of reports your vicinity, period. Wind* **east southeast** *about twenty five knots* (28.8 mph) *to* (ship) <u>*Ontario then* (reversing)</u> *east* **to east northeast** *about 20 knots* (23 mph) *to Howland.*" - Fleet Base Pearl Harbour."[lvi]

The report was warning that beginning at the *SS Ontario* they would be flying through the normally out of play Inter-Tropical Convergence Zone. It is typically located about **4° north** of the equator. But Pearl Harbor reported the wind change at *Ontario's* position which was **2°59' south** of the equator. This was a **6.6** degree latitudinal difference. Their flight plan was now fatally flawed.

Fred and Amelia had departed without this critical reverse wind weather update. They had trimmed the plane for an east north-easterly destination in a 28 mph headwind on their front right (starboard) side.

At destination, "Three emergency runways had been constructed on the island by the U.S. Government with no other apparent purpose than receiving the Earhart plane."[lvii] "Howland Island is just <u>two degrees north</u> of the equator some 2,575 miles southwest of Honolulu, Hawaii. Today it is an unincorporated area administered by the U.S. Fish and Wildlife Service…and the U.S. Department of the Interior."[lviii] The 1937 landing strip is no longer serviceable.

Amelia and Fred settled in to fly east all day and night across two time zones into the next sunrise. They must have felt alone as they plowed ahead with nothing but the sky's vastness, the Pacific Ocean's endless 360-degree ocean horizon, and the plane's roaring radial engines. The flight was to take approximately eighteen hours. But unknown as they passed the *Ontario's* position, cloud cover set in that was a time zone wide.

At 5:00 p.m. local time, Earhart radioed Lae City Airport that the plane was at 7,000 feet (2.1km) and was making 150 mph (241kph). Seven hours and twenty minutes after their departure, Earhart had only covered 785 miles, which meant their air speed had been approximately 123 mph (198kph). "That longitude reading meant that the headwinds they were encountering were stronger than had been predicted."[lix] At this rate, their estimated four hour fuel reserve would be reduced. But, that would not be a problem as long as they were on course.

- **Earhart Radio** - 5:20 p.m.: *Position 4.33 south 159.7 east. Height 8000 feet over cumulus clouds. Wind 23 knots* (26.5 mph).[ix]

Their fuel consumption was only moving the plane an average of 118 miles per hour (190 kph), not at the normal 150 mph (241kph) pace.

- **Earhart Radio** - 10:30 p.m. *A ship in sight ahead.*

United States Coast Guard
The United States Naval "auxiliary tug" USS *Ontario.*

The timing was right. The *Ontario* was at anchor 1278 miles (2057km) from the Lae City Airport, approximately half way to Howland Island at 2.6° south latitude. But because notification was delayed, *Ontario's* radioman did not broadcast as requested, nor did the men listen for a plane that night. "Near the middle of the night Lieutenant Blakeslee of the *Ontario*, a coal burning beacon ship from Samoa on station midway between Lae and Howland, noted that <u>a frontal system had moved in</u>."[lxi] Pearl Harbor's prediction was correct. The convergence zone was confirmed at 6.6 degrees south of where it is normally encountered. The *Ontario* departed for Pago Pago two hours after the over flight time.

"Southeast trade winds blowing at twenty-five miles per hour were the norm in June, according to Clarence S. Williams, who mapped portions of the flight."[lxii] It was July 1st. As their head-winds shifted from southeast to northeast, properly corrected rudder trim adjustments became mission critical. Because of McMoneagle, we now know this did not happen.

As their plane slowly lost fuel weight, in 20-25 knot (23.5-

28.8mph) diagonal headwinds, updated drift adjustments were essential to stay on course. But their situation - in total darkness - included: **(1)** a strong reversed wind system; **(2)** severely reduced communications and; **(3)** cloud cover preventing starlit navigation. This was a worst-case scenario for finding a speck of land in the Pacific Ocean. They needed celestial bearings, but could not get them due to high altitude cloud cover. Eventually they climbed to 12,000 feet, but were still unable to get their bearings.

**McMoneagle** – (Once passed the SS *Ontario*) **I think they were fighting a head wind that was hitting them a little bit off their port** (left) **side; it probably drove them further to the south than they anticipated. It was probably not enough to register on the type of wind direction devices they had at the time...**

Off Howland Island, and in position since June 23, the USCG *Itasca's* radio communications with Earhart were sketchy. There are four versions. There is the original report, and the revised report written three days later when officers realized this was going all the way to the Roosevelts in the White House. There was *Itasca's* Commander Warner G. Thompson's report of July 19, 1937, entitled *Radio Transcripts Earhart Flight*. And there is *Itasca's* original log as first notated by the chief radioman and kept in the U. S. National Archives. There are discrepancies in all four.

As Earhart got closer, the radiomen stood by for contact. What they received is presented chronologically. All time stamps are ship's time.

**- Earhart Radio** - 02:45-48 a.m.: *Cloudy weather. Cloudy*. Itasca's Captain, Warner K. Thompson, later reported she said: "C*loudy and overcast*."

The *Itasca* transmitted at 3:00 and 3:30 a.m. as scheduled. They received no response until...

**- Earhart Radio** - 03:45 a.m.: *Itasca from Earhart. Itasca broadcast on 3105 kilocycles on hour and half-hour - repeat - broadcast on 3105 kilocycles on hour and half hour. Overcast.*

At this point engineers speculated Amelia and Fred were 500 nautical miles from Howland Island. They should arrive in about four hours. But Amelia reported they were flying in cloudy and overcast skies. We now know Fred was prevented from getting navigational bearings the entire night. As the plane drifted hundreds of miles south of their flight plan, Noonan certainly would have made adjustments had he known their position.

- **Earhart Radio** – 04:54 a.m.: *Partly cloudy*. It has been speculated this meant Noonan could now get a starlight bearing. But we now know that did not happen. Noonan was not able to get an updated position until after dawn.

**McMoneagle - Visibility is bad, with a rather thick and stormy cloud front that is sitting about 1,100 feet off the deck. More like early morning fog off water than actual clouds really. I think as fuel ran low, they tried to make contact with the place they were going to, but were unable to do so. I get a strong sense that the frequencies were screwed up, or they were each trying to talk on different frequencies from each other. They were in communication, but only sporadically. I don't think they ever clearly heard anyone actually, just voices lost in static.**

The radio continued to be mostly unintelligible as four to five sailors listened. But with reduced fuel, meaningful communication became critical. The radiomen sent a weather report and requested flight position at 5:00, 5:30 and 6:00 a.m.

- **Earhart Radio** – 06:14 a.m. (still dark) *Want bearings on 3105 kilocycles on hour. Will whistle in microphone.* Then, one minute later: *Almost two hundred miles out. Whistling now.*

This distance has confused researchers ever since. We now know it was based on travel time, not navigational coordinates. And now, *Itasca* was to provide the homing signals.

Fred Noonan was one of the world's best navigators who found himself in unexpected reverse head winds in heavy cloud cover. In the original flight plan, the Tropical Convergence Zone was not considered in play as it was normally 2° north of Howland Island. So normally those updated rudder trim adjustments would not needed until the next day's flight.

Sunrise was at 6:36 that morning with the sun rising at 67° true. *Itasca's* radiomen asked for a position at 6:30 a.m. Still cloudy, we know now Earhart was crossing Howland Island's longitude toward the Carondelet Reef. Its north edge is 66 miles (106km) southeast of Nikumaroro Atoll at 5°34′S-173°51′W. It is approximately one mile (1.5km) in length. With the rising water in the 21st Century it is about 1.8 meters (5.9 feet) below the water's surface.

- **Earhart Radio** – 06:45 a.m.: *Please take bearing on us and* *report in half hour - I will make noise in microphone about 100 miles out.*

Again, Amelia's comment about being *"100 miles out"* was based on Fred's time line. And ever since, historians have been led astray by the *Itasca's* north of the equator weather log which read: "*Clear skies with detached clouds.*" But as night slipped into day, we now know their plane was hundreds of miles south south-east of the ship. *Itasca's* radiomen transmitted at 7:00, 7:18 and 7:30 a.m. as Fred finally got his bearings.

**McMoneagle – They realized they had missed their primary destination when they were approximately 50 minutes overdue and made a decision at that point --- which was pretty much an accurate one — that they were somewhere south of the primary destination. There seems to be a lot of confusion with regard to communications, and the pilot is changing course drastically. Essentially turning and flying in a north–northwest direction, which she feels will ultimately bring them to a place they can set the plane down.**

**They made the turn based on sandbars they were seeing and guessing that a small island they passed an hour earlier to their southeast was a group of islands to the south-east of where they were heading. I think they checked a map and saw that there was a very <u>high probability of hitting an island</u> by turning to the northwest or west-northwest. It was a solid calculation. I think a good bet.**

**I get a sense that they are crossing over what appears to be a series of small reefs that are just breaking the surface of the water** (low tide in 1937). **I see what appears to be a section of "U" shaped reefs or islands, which are south of a group of reefs or islands that are in the shape of an "E" to the north. I think they made a turn about an hour and fifteen minutes prior to running out of fuel.**

<u>Feedback Inquiry</u>: *It almost seems impossible Noonan did not know they were south of the equator when they were supposed to be north of it. I was wondering if there was any sense of this.*

**McMoneagle – If they were flying at 1,000 feet, then there was no way he could have** (been) **taking any kind of a sighting, except very generally as the sun would have been very obscured by clouds, or at best intermittent through the clouds.**

After reviewing his calculations, Fred Noonan looked over at the fuel gauge and realized they would not make Howland Island. He told Amelia to turn the plane around. They had enough reserves to make it back to the correct longitude. Fred now had to decide what to say. Her radio messages indicate she thought Howland Island would be there when they got back to the correct longitudinal line.

A review of **_cockpit dynamics_** points to Fred attempting to avoid conflict with Amelia. With his calculations, he realized they were ~4.5 degrees south of the equator. Then after looking at the fuel gauge Noonan realized: **(1)** the World Flight would not be a success; **(2)** they may have to ditch at sea; **(3)** he wanted to delay any emotional upset in the cockpit.

Fred must have told Amelia that they had passed the longitude and they would be approaching Howland Island from the east. He led Amelia to believe everything would be okay on this reversed heading. They had enough fuel to make it back, so this reassurance held their rapport together for most of another hour.

Feedback Inquiry: *Did you get any sense Fred Noonan was aware they would not make Howland Island during that last hour of flight?*

**McMoneagle - I believe he knew based on the <u>duration</u> of the flight time, and whatever dead reckoning he was able to do...following dawn that they had missed the island and it was somewhere to their north, northwest, necessitating the turn in that direction... He probably thought he had a fairly good fix on where they were, but when they got to where they** (Amelia) **thought they should have been, there was nothing there they** (she) **expected to find.**

Upon returning to the 157-337 longitudinal line, *Itasca* received a critical message confirming our new interpretation.

**- Earhart Radio** – 07:42 a.m.: *Calling Itasca.* (Based on Fred) *We must be on you, but cannot see you, but gas is running low. Been unable to reach you by radio. We are flying at a 1000 feet.*

# Evidential Details

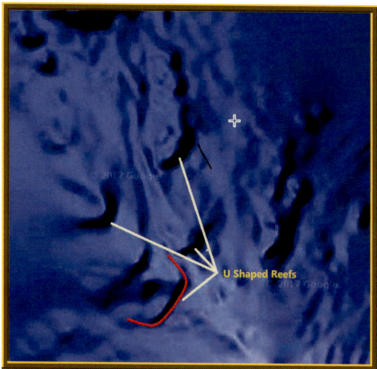

Google Earth 3D ©2017

**McMoneagle - I see what appears to be a section of "U" shaped reefs...which are south of a group of reefs...that are in the shape of an "E" to the north.**

McMoneagle's drawings (right) were used to locate the reefs. The above image is from the Carondelet Reef. These are the reefs south of the E shaped reefs, which are shown on the facing page. The sharp corner reef (red outline) is likely the one drawn and is probably the flight's turning point.

A fly over is needed to see if more detailed pictures can be taken.

McMoneagle RV Art – *Evidential Details* ©1998

# Amelia Earhart

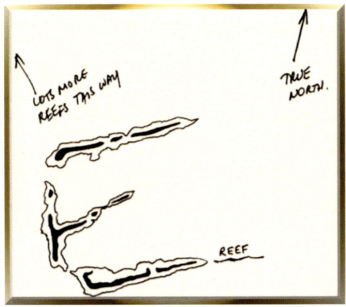

Top - McMoneagle RV Art – Evidential Details ©1998    Below - ©Google Earth 3D 2012

Drawn 14 years before they were discovered, from 18,316 feet, the fingers of McMoneagle's capital **E** shaped reefs emerged north of the **U** shaped reefs.

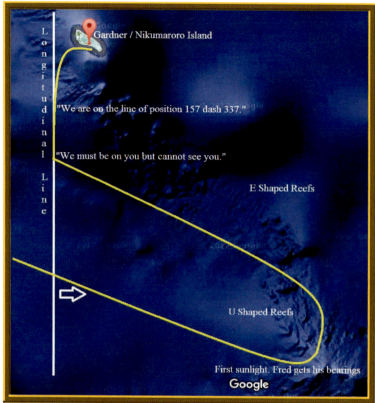

Google Earth 3D 2017

The flight's unknown 2nd half went into the Carondelet Reef. Their northwest adjustment turned at the "**U Shaped**" reefs. They banked northwest through the capital "**E Shaped**" reefs to return to the 157 – 337 longitude leading north to Howland Island. Their last received radio message was when they were northbound on the line before they were forced to ditch at Nikumaroro/Gardner Island.

**Cockpit dynamics**: We now know the statement: *"We must be on you, but cannot see you"* at 7:42 a.m. confirms our Noonan scenario. They were actually about 400 miles south of *SS Itasca*. So this clarifies that Fred led Amelia to believe Howland Island would be there when they got back to the longitudinal line.

The *Itasca* transmitted at 7:43, 7:47, and 7:49 a.m.

**- Earhart Radio** - 07:58 a.m.: *We are listening but cannot see* (Howland) *island. Cannot hear you. Go ahead on 7500 kilocycles with long count either now or on schedule time on half hour.*

**Cockpit dynamics**: Sixteen minutes later Amelia still believed she should be over Howland Island. She is surprised she cannot hear anything when she is above the *Itasca*. Fred does not let on. He

First publicized here, the Intertropical Convergence Zone's and Earhart's flight path are mapped. This area to the right of the **maroon line** was an overcast cloud bank. Earhart's flight path went past the ***S.S. Ontario*** (yellow arch top). As the Zone pushed southwest, the winds reversed from southeast to northeast (blue arrows). By sun-up Earhart had past Howland Island's longitude (top right circle). They turned back (orange line center right) and turned north on the longitudinal line until they came upon the Nikumaroro Atoll. The grey arrow (right side) is where Amelia radioed "*we must be on you but cannot see you.*"

tells her to continue north on the longitudinal line privately hoping they will run into an opportunity to survive

**McMoneagle - Get a sense that when the island they were flying to didn't show up in front of them within 30 minutes of the** (Fred's) **appointed time that would have cause a rise in stress. They thought** (Fred said) **they were probably only about 120 to 150 kilometers** (75–93 miles) **to the south** (of Howland Island)**, which of course was wrong...**

After correctly calculating the remaining fuel, Fred's statement purchased harmony for the rest of the flight. That distance was the extent of their time aloft.

**- Earhart Radio -** 08:00 a.m.: *Earhart calling Itasca. We received your signals but unable to get minimum. Please take bearings on us and answer on 3105 kilocycles with voice.*

In the time since 7:42 a.m. Amelia may have begun to think something was not right. Fred had always been on target. The airplane transmitted dashes to *Itasca* "for a brief period" on 3105 kilocycles. The result was that the *Itasca* was unable to determine the aircraft's position.

**McMoneagle - In searching forward in time, I get a sense of great stress... This may simply be a sense that it is the ultimate range of their particular type of plane... I think he** (Noonan) **had a damned good idea and they just simply ran out of gas, otherwise they probably would have made it.**

Fred knew where he was. For comparison, during their flight from Hawaii to Oakland, CA. Fred took seven radio bearings, 14 star or planet positions and nine navigational fixes, leading to four course corrections. None of this had happened on the way to Howland Island. So it is the next communication that has baffled researchers ever since. It has been thought that Earhart was flying back and forth - north and south - on the longitudinal line. However, with our insight, it was time for a major reinterpretation of their next message.

*Itasca* transmitted nine times before Amelia was next understood. Fred had given Amelia coordinates in his navigational north/south idiom. And 43 minutes later, a message got through:

**- Earhart Radio** – 08:43-4 a.m. – *We are on the line of position 157 dash 337. Will repeat this message on 6210 kilocycles. We are **now** running north and south. Heading north and south ... We are running on...line.*

**Cockpit dynamics**: Fred provided Amelia with the coordinates. Two things emerge: **(1)** the word "*now*" is a clue that has been hiding in plain sight ever since. It means they were on line at this time. It confirms they had *returned* to the line. **(2)** Fred had only provided her with longitudinal data. He could not provide latitudinal coordinates without giving away their position.

*Running north and south* is Fred's navigational jargon spoken by Amelia. They were not flying back and forth on reverse direction headings (TIGHAR's Theory). In order to think this, you <u>must</u> believe Fred could not determine if he was north or south of the equator as they continued north into open skies!

The Itasca transmitted at 8:47 a.m. with no response. As the plane approached Nikumaroro from the south, their radio signal strength was said to be at a maximum level of S5. Challenged by the TIGHAR Group, this signal strength has led researchers to conclude the plane was very close to Howland Island.

**- *Earhart Radio*** – *08:55 a.m.* (Twenty minutes of fuel remaining) - *We are running on line north and south.*

**McMoneagle - After about an hour and ten minutes to probably about an hour and fifteen minutes, they spotted reefs** (Nikumaroro Atoll) **just above the water line, but could not see any islands. I do not sense any kind of an island with anything that is very tall, like a mountain or anything like that.**

**Very low on fuel, they decided to take a chance on landing** (in the water) **instead of flying on to their final destination. I have a very strong sense that they** (he) **actually knew where they were, or at least approximately, but just plain ran out of fuel. I do not believe they were successful in passing along their estimated location or the fact that they were ditching, but <u>believed</u> at the time that they had been heard and understood.**

**Get a strong sense of exhaustion. I get a very strong feeling of failure, but not because of threat or possible loss of life, but more because of some larger failure of some sort, maybe more of a personal one.**

There was reason for this. Amelia had real concern for her supporters as this aircraft was a loaner. Ostensibly, the airplane was an Alumni donation made to Purdue University's Aeronautical Research Fund. In addition, George Putnam had spent $34,000 ($622,828/2020) for repairs when Amelia crashed in Hawaii that

March. She realized she would have to face her husband's frustration because the book he was writing was to recoup those repair costs. Then there were the Roosevelts who had publically given their support. Amelia also had commercial sponsorships including her line of luggage.

With all this, we began to realize her beaching approach reflected a desire to preserve the airplane as intact as possible. This investment was to be returned to the Purdue University Research Foundation. "Income realized from the book and exhibitions of the plane were to be used to advance applied research in aeronautics."[lxiii] Also, Fred must have been concerned about being the fall guy. Navigation had gone wrong and he knew Palmer Putnam had opposed his involvement from the start.

**McMoneagle – I also get a very good attitude, as though they fully expect to not have any trouble ditching. It is almost a routine feeling, as though it won't be any trouble and that everything will be okay, and it won't be long before they are picked up. There was no panic. Too professional for that.**

During our feedback sessions, this satellite picture (next page) was e-mailed to McMoneagle. Did he have any comments?

**McMoneagle – Just that they would have probably been approaching the atoll from the bottom left of the frame; more than likely from just about the height shown in the picture.**

What happened next is also unknown. It is lays to rest to many legends, debates and books. Earhart's mysterious vanishing was in part resolved by the timing of the ocean tides.

The Nikumaroro Atoll has a 300–350-foot wide (91-107m) coral reef around its edges. At low tide, it is broad and flat adding many acres to the island. In 1937, the closest tidal records were kept at Orona (Hull) Island some 165 miles (265k) east. The United Kingdom's Easy Tide offices indicated that Hull Island's low tide was at 7:43 a.m. on Friday July 2, 1937.[lxiv] There is a ten-minute tidal delay between the two islands making Nikumaroro's low tide at approximately 7:53 a.m.

This fit with McMoneagle's post 9:00 a.m. arrival time. The passing of +70 minutes for the low tide to rise up to reef level, and then rising another 12–18 inches (35-45cm) above the reef, matched the timing constraint. According to Tom King PhD., the low tide drops approximately one yard below the reef's edge.[lxv]

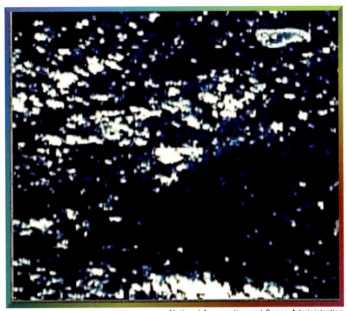

National Aeronautics and Space Administration
Gardner Island/Nikumaroro (above) is what McMoneagle interpreted as reefs.
It is on Howland Island's longitude. Descending bottom left to top right, after
23+ hours in the air, imagine their relief with the fuel gauge reading *Empty*.

Earhart's approach was when the tide had just covered the
Atoll's coral shelf. The reef then became a dangerously concealed
obstacle. Amelia and Fred would literally be flying into a cliff or
what is the top of an invisible underwater volcanic butte. As she
faced east into the morning sun, there was a glare on the water.

**McMoneagle – Sending maydays on a specific com-
munications frequency, but get a sense that it was too high
for the normal SOS calls. Having monitored for SOS's in ship-
ping, I know that this frequency is usually very low. I believe
the frequency they were operating on was much higher. That
also would have affected the type of direction finding equipment this plane was carrying as well, which is probably a
loop, maybe a foot or 3/4's of a foot in diameter.[11]**

**Wheels up. Both nervous, both knowing they are
making a forced landing with almost no fuel left in what they
hope will be shallow water next to (Nikumaroro's) a reef line.
They expected to slip along the surface of the water. They**

---

[11] Mr. McMoneagle has a military license in radio communications and Morse Code.

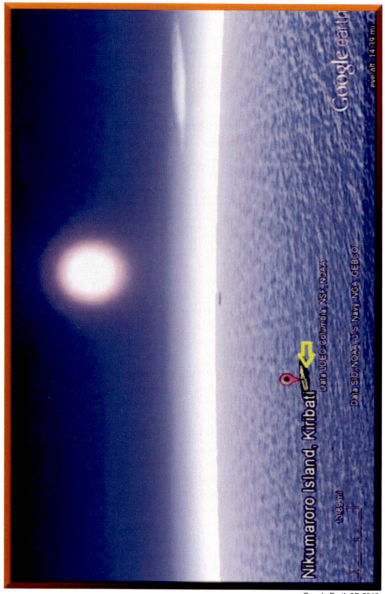

Google Earth 3D 2013

# The Gardner/Nikumaroro Atoll

Earhart's likely view looking east from Howland Island's 157 – 337 longitudinal line. They were into the morning sun's glare as she attempted to save as much of the aircraft as possible on the island's southeast end (yellow arrow). Orona (Hull Island) can just be seen on the horizon below the sun.

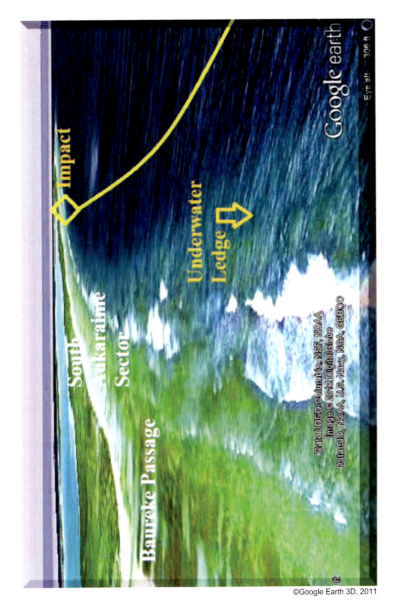

©Google Earth 3D, 2011

# The Hidden Coral Shelf

Starting at the underwater reef ledge (aqua colored water), by nine a.m. the tidal advance was too high to attempt a landing on the now partially concealed reef shelf. The yellow line approximates her attempt to nestle the plane into the curvature. When she set down, the coral reef stopped her plane like flying into a concrete abutment, as the left (port) wing hit first turning the plane into the coral shelf.

75

kept the wheels up for that purpose. They didn't make a run or pass first, probably afraid to waste what little fuel they had left. Get a sense the engines were already giving them trouble, might have even had one quit on them, which means they were adjusting the trim radically, fighting the pull of the single engine. Came in about as perfect as one could expect, touched water, bounced once, touched down again, and for about two seconds, very pleased with the result. It was a mistake.

Suddenly—SLAM.

There is...what appears to be a crash. They hit a coral head the plane stops sharply in the water...the belly of the plane hit a coral out cropping and it stopped dead in the water ripping out the belly plates. ...they are both slammed forward against the dash (and) interior sections of the plane coming apart.

She probably attempted to land in the water between outside reefs, attempting to use the calmer water and preserve as much of her ship as possible. Coming to such an abrupt stop, folded the wings forward, probably ripping at least an engine off with a wing just from their weight and being suddenly brought to a complete and sudden stop. Get a sense the left engine separated with a section of wing and drove itself into the coral bank, tearing the port side of the plane apart. The tail then came up and over the top, turning the aircraft over. It hits upside down. Both passengers are unconscious, bleeding from facial and head wounds. The plane fills with water in what appears to be half a minute or less and sinks quickly below the waves. Both passengers drown and never feel a thing.

Cockpit dynamics: As the seat belted passengers were crushed against the cockpit dash at about 85 mph (137k/h). Everything in the cockpit was blown through the cabin windows. This accounts for personal items found decades later as well as items found by Gerry Gallagher, as well as the cockpit's Plexiglas window pieces.

The plane's belly collided at about the landing light level. The tail came up all the way over the top and the plane slid into the water upside down. It rolled down to an underwater ridge who's denied sea floor topography was first confirmed in 2012 at the location and depth of about 650-feet (198m). The off shore place is where McMoneagle indicated on his 1998 report map (next page).

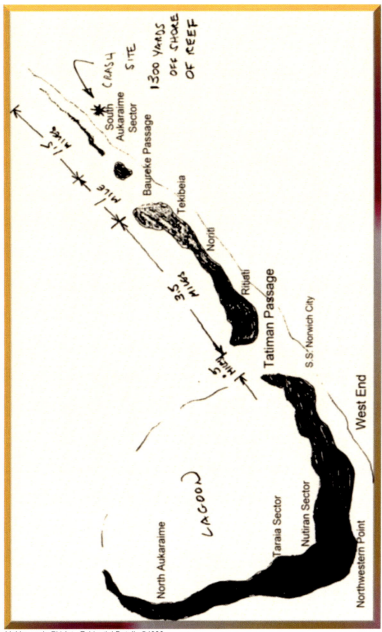

McMoneagle RV Art - Evidential Details ©1998

# Location Map

With nine geographic points identified, this is the Operation Star Gate
map that would have supplied to Pentagon for Earhart mystery analysts.

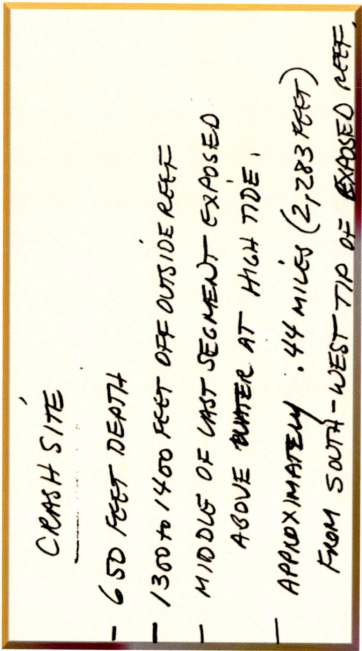

CRASH SITE

6 SO FEET DEPTH

130 to 140 FEET OFF OUTSIDE REEF

MIDDLE OF LAST SEGMENT EXPOSED

ABOVE BUNKER AT HIGH TIDE,

APPROXIMATELY .44 MILES (2,283 FEET)

FROM SOUTH-WEST TIP OF EXPOSED REEF

McMoneagle RV Artwork – Evidential Details ©1998
    Joseph McMoneagle's Pentagon grade debris field data. Neutral, third
party feedback will be the key to determining these number's final accuracy.

©2017 Google Earth 3D

Gardner Island's southeast end showing the roll down trajectory. The oval debris field sits just in front of the light colored rise shown in the water. In 2012 a ridge was discovered here that prevented the plane from rolling to the ocean floor.

**McMoneagle** – I think they tried to land either very close to one of the above water reefs, or close to a small sand bar off to the <u>east</u> of one of the reefs, but this has ended in disaster. They try and hit the water knowing it is too dangerous to actually try and land on the reefs or sand. But in trying to do so, the plane essentially just folds up on a coral head, which is located just under the surface of the water, flipping itself over, and breaking up in the surface chop, and the plane sinks rapidly to the bottom. I would put it at about 9:00 to 9:30 (a.m.) **give or take about a half-hour.** It was about 9:15am.

Actual site of the ditching is marked on the map with a symbol (asterisk) of an airplane. The location is probably generally accurate if matched to major features in the area but there are a lot of reefs (Nikumaroro's southern coast') and sandbars here, which would not probably be on a map.

I think…it is all lying within a circle with a <u>radius of</u>

**about 75 yards**. I think there are <u>lots of parts</u> still there. **Given a proper map to scale for this area (wherever it is) I can dowse the map and perhaps tell you within a quarter mile of where it lies. Get a sense that this is a tropical place based on the trees; there are no trees where the plane went down by the way. The map would have to show topographical features for sandbars and reefs, even when they are not very high above sea level, in order to do this**

So, are there any details to prove Earhart's airplane was ever at this location? When it comes to Nikumaroro artifact retrieval, there has been the airplane parts vs. Earhart's personal items vs. the 13 years of colonist refuse conundrum.

Many Nikumaroro Island artifacts remain controversial. But the TIGHAR Group has made it worse insisting everything proved their personalized Castaways theory. None of their objects proves any post-crash human behavior. So our investigation eliminated this confusion by separating personal effects from aviation parts.

Lockheed's Electra 10 was in production from 1934 to 1941. It was considered the finest ten seat plane of its day. The E series was set up for freight – in this case the aircraft was built for bulk liquids transport (aviation fuel) without passenger windows.

# The Evidence

It became time to give credit where credit was due. There have been aircraft parts discovered at Nikumaroro by the TIGHAR Group. Historians will recall the repairs made after Amelia's Wheeler AFB crash in March of 1937. At that time updated parts and different airframe riveting was introduced that were at variance with Lockheed design specifications. Here is a review of three parts recovered at Nikumaroro.

<u>Item 1</u>: **Electra 10 windshield pieces** – On January 15, 1937 Lockheed reduced the Electra's cockpit Plexiglas thickness specification from **5/32** to **1/8** inch. Some 75 days later Earhart's repaired Electra was the first to install this **updated part**. Two Plexiglas pieces were recovered at Nikumaroro. Their thickness matched the updated windshield Part# 40552. Quote: *"Lockheed engineering drawings show that the material, the curvature, and the thickness of the artifact match those specified for the cabin windows of the Electra. The curvature and thickness of the Plexiglas found on*

*Nikumaroro exactly matches Lockheed's specifications for Electra cabin windows at exactly the time Earhart's new windows were installed."[xvi]*

Amelia Earhart's crash in March, 1937 at Wheeler Air Force Base, Hawaii.

**Item 2:** **Ripped and torn fuselage metal** - Aluminum skin was recovered cracked and ripped with torn rivet holes verifying extreme force according to the National Transportation Safety Board review: *"This is a forcibly removed section (of) aluminum which was once part of an airplane skin."*

As per Lockheed's completed Repair Orders signed off on April 19, 1937, it was indicated those pieces matched a repair patch on the underside of Earhart's airplane: *"...the NTSB did note that the fracture geometry along the line of 5/32 rivet holes is consistent with (metal) tearing separations..."*

Additionally, there are 3/32 inch rivet holes on this fuselage piece. Lockheed did not use both rivet spacings, but Earhart's belly repair patches did to enhance strength. Ripping and tearing metal are not forces Micronesian colonists could bring to bear on metal. As the only Electra 10 to have this repair by June 1937, the NTSB concluded the artifact appeared to be from Earhart's plane. The question is how did these artifacts get to Nikumaroro if not flown in? Why are they smashed, broken, ripped and torn?

Next came the March 28, 2014 report from the Restoration Division Staff at the United States Air Force National Museum at Wright-Patterson AFB in Ohio. They reviewed the same TIGHAR artifact# 2-2-V-1 the NTSB previously reviewed. They concluded:

Author

The riveted rectangular panels on the Lockheed Electra 10. This is where consider-able crash reconstruction work took place four months before her flight. All Electra 10 histories are known, and none had dual rivet belly patch repairs by 1937.

**Point 1** – *"The sheet is made of a product introduced by Alcoa Aluminum in 1933 known as "24ST Alclad." Earhart's Lockheed 10E Special was skinned with 24ST Alclad";*

**Point 2** - The artifact is a piece forcibly separated from a larger panel of aluminum aircraft skin; and, *"The artifact is, without question, from an aircraft that suffered catastrophic damage some-where in the Central South Pacific region. At present, of the known losses in the Central South Pacific, only Earhart's Electra fits all of the requirements;"*

**Point 3** – *"The sheet is perforated with four rows of rivet holes 3/32" in diameter with a precise pitch* (interval between holes) *of 1". One edge of the sheet failed along a staggered double row of rivet holes 5/32" in diameter with irregular pitch."* And, *"These irregularities suggest that* (part) *2-2-V-1 may be part of a repair."*

**Point 4** – *"Most of the rivets failed in tension when a fluid force struck the sheet on the interior surface with sufficient energy to* <u>*blow the heads off the rivets*</u>.*"*

**Point 5** – *"Because the artifact was found on Nikumaroro, it fol-lows that the aircraft-of-origin was a type that was present at some time in that part of the world. Due to the remoteness of the Central*

*South Pacific* (in 1937)*, those aircraft types are a limited and known population."* [lxvii]

With their report the Castaways Theory faded even further. **Item 3: Electrical Cord** – A ten strand electrical cord was discovered at Nikumaroro/Gardener Island. The plugs at each end connected a 1930's Bendix electrical generator with a General Electric radio plug. Earhart's plane used both pieces of equipment.

Originally, the wreck's 650 foot (198m) ocean depth seemed strange and left us wondering why the fuselage would not roll down to the ocean floor. But through dedicated after hours work, an underwater ridge was discovered during the July, 2012 Nikumaroro expedition by Dr. J.R. Smith and PhDs from the U. of H.'s Hawaiian Underwater Research Laboratory (HURL) team.

In the fourth quarter of 2012, certain members of the TIGHAR Group's Internet Forum cautiously concluded what we had indicated since the fourth quarter of 1998. They suggested, "*She was never there*" as a castaway, meaning the plane was never within TIGHAR's format. The problem was that, until our scenario, no one had a solid alternative.

# Aftermath

When Amelia's plane did not arrive, the Press sang out:

*EARHART DOWN IN PACIFIC*
*EARHART DISAPPEARS*
*AMELIA'S PLANE VANISHES*
*PACIFIC CLAIMS EARHART* [lxviii]

On the fourth of July, 1937 Naval District Commander, Admiral Orrin G. Murfin, ordered Jonathan S. Dowell, Captain in overall command of the Lexington Aircraft Carrier Task Force, to sail to the search area where a week long hunt ensued. "For the next thirty days, the nation talked about little else. The search for Amelia and Fred was the largest and most expensive in U.S. history involving nine ships, 66 aircraft and well over 4,000 sailors. At the request of President Franklin Roosevelt (1882-1945), the Navy sent the carrier *Lexington*, battleship *Colorado*, and a dozen other vessels."[lxix] "Joining immediately with the *Lex* were the destroyers *Drayton*, *Lamson*, and *Cushing*, the fuel tanker *Ramapo*, and the mine sweeper *Swan*."[lxx]

Early on husband George Putnam suspected the due south Phoenix Island group. Knowing he had the White House behind him, he contacted the stateside Navy as well as Captain Wilhelm L. Friedell on the battleship *USS Colorado*:

George Putnam telegram - July 6, 1937 - *Please note all radio bearings thus far obtained on Earhart plane approximately intersect in Phoenix Island region southeast of Howland island period. Further line of position given by Noonan if based on Howland which apparently reasonable assumption also passes through islands period. Therefore, suggested that planes from Colorado investigate Phoenix area as practicable unquote.*[lxxi]

Then on July 7, World War II technically began when the Japanese Army clashed with Chinese forces near Peiping, China.

On July 9, at 7:00 a.m. three spotter planes were catapulted from the *USS Colorado* to fly over the Phoenix Islands includeing Gardner (Nikumaroro) Island. They found nothing (p. 97 & 98).

On July 12, the Japanese Ambassador contacted the U.S. State Department announcing Japan had two ships taking part in the search for Amelia Earhart.

On July 13, the first 60 planes from the carrier *Lexington* were launched. Unfortunately the search went north of Howland Island. Nine war ships and sixty-six airplanes became involved at a cost of more than $4 million ($73m/2020). Some 150,000 sq. miles (388,498sq.km) of ocean were searched. Amelia and Fred had vanished and one of America's greatest mysteries began. But George Putnam got more involved. At this point, he turned to one of Amelia's aviation friends - Jackie Cochran.[12]

In 1936 Amelia and Jackie had spent time together. Preeminent Earhart author Mary Lovell: "Over Christmas, Amelia and Jackie spent a great deal of time discussing aviation, but, in particular, they shared an interest in mental telepathy and psychic phenomena. They evidently put their interest to some practical use..." "Quite what to make of these claims, so unlike the practical,

---

[12] Jacqueline Cochran (1910-1980) was an award-winning pilot in her own right. In 1937, she was the only woman to fly in the Bendix Transcontinental Air Race taking third place. Starting in 1938, for three years straight, she won the Clifford Burke Harmon Trophy as the world's outstanding woman. In 1939, she set the woman's altitude record. In 1940, she set two aviation world speed records. She was awarded the Distinguished Service Medal In 1945. In 1953, she was the first woman to break the sound barrier.

even prosaic Amelia, is difficult, and becomes more so in the light of subsequent events."[lxxii]

According to Lovell, on December 15, 1936, Amelia called the Western Air Express Company (merged with American Airlines in 2001) about one of their downed planes. She told them a trapper had looted their aircraft. An individual subsequently turned up in Salt Lake City talking about the downed airplane, but left before he could be questioned.

Then again, in just under two weeks Amelia called United Airlines on December 27, advising the management where to find a scheduled flight that had crashed. "The wreckage was duly found in the location she had given them." Two weeks later, she called to advise Western Airlines (merged with Delta in 1987) of the position of one of their downed charter planes. "It was found fifteen miles north of Burbank, California, just where she said it would be."[lxxiii] Now George Putnam called Jackie Cochran and others at the Psychic Research Society for help with Amelia's disappearance.

Remembering what Amelia and Jackie had done earlier, Putnam considered her information accurate enough to pursue it officially. On July 17, he withheld his source when he sent new search coordinates to the *U.S.S. Lexington's* Captain Noyes. But: *"...because* (of the) *peculiar intimate nature* (of the) *alleged information this is a confidential personal request to you."*

With no response, in just under 17 hours, he inquired again re-stating that the crash site coordinates which: *"...for intimate reasons one cannot rationalize or wisely make public."*[lxxiv]

Nothing was found and on July 19, the naval search was discontinued. But Putnam would not give up. He took his request to Cabinet level people in the Roosevelt Administration - in this case Commerce Secretary Daniel Roper:

George Putnam telegram - July 23, 1937 – *Whatever it may be possible to do will be appreciated. For your confidential information extraordinary evidence seems to exist indicating castaway still living though of such strange nature cannot be officially publicly confirmed.*[lxxv]

Thus, in 1937, history's first allusion to castaways was made by an unscientifically tested, non-military, California psychic enthusiast group.

On January 5, 1939, George Palmer Putnam (1887-1950)

took possession of Amelia's estate when the probate court ruled she was dead, and married Jean Marie Cosigny. In 1944, he divorced her and married Margaret Haviland. "In December 1949 he became very ill and was taken to Trona Hospital in Trona, California, where he died (age 63) at 6:05 a.m., on January 4, 1950, from internal hemorrhages and uremic poisoning."[lxxvi] This was apparently from complications after eating poison meat during his search for Amelia in Burma (Myanmar).[lxxvii]

Given her sense of personal reality, Amelia would appreciate that the world's first decorated military intelligence remote viewer solved her mystery. She had not grown old and had "*popped off*" with the type death she foretold: "*in my airplane, quickly.*"

# Earhart Chronology

• October, 1922 - Set women's 14,000 foot altitude record;

• June, 1928 - First woman to passenger across the Atlantic Ocean in 20 hours and 40 minutes in the Fokker F7, Friendship airplane;

• August, 1929 – Took Third Place in the First Women's Air Derby; Earhart then upgraded from her Avian airplane to the Lockheed Vega;

• Fall, 1929 - Elected as an official for the National Aeronautic Association and encouraged the Federation Aeronautique Internationale (FAI) to establish separate world altitude, speed and endurance records for women;

• June, 1930 - Set women's speed record for 100 kilometers unloaded, and with a load of 500 kilograms (1102 lbs).

• July, 1930 - Speed record set of 181.18 mph over a 300K (186 mile) course;

• 1931 - Speed record for 100 km with 500 lb. (227kg) load;

• April, 1931 – First woman to fly and set woman's altitude record of 18,415 feet (5.61km) in a Pitcairn autogiro;

• May, 1932 - First woman to fly solo across the Atlantic in 15 hours, 18 minutes on the 5th anniversary of Charles Lindberg's Trans-Atlantic flight; awarded National Geographic Society's gold medal (p.121) from President Herbert Hoover (1874-1964); awarded the Distinguished Flying Cross from the United States Congress (p. 91); First woman to fly the Atlantic Ocean twice;

- August, 1932 - First woman to fly solo nonstop U.S. coast to coast; set women's nonstop transcontinental speed record, flying 2,447.8 miles (3,939.35km) in 19 hours and 5 minutes;
- Fall, 1932 - Elected president of the Ninety Nines, a new women's aviation club which she helped to form;
- 1932 - First person to cross the U.S. in an auto gyro;
- July, 1933 - Broke her previous transcontinental speed record by two hours making the flight in 17 hours and 7 minutes;
- January,1935 - First person to solo the 2,408-mile (3,875.3km) distance across the Pacific Ocean between Honolulu and Oakland, California; also was the first civilian flight to carry a two-way radio;
- May, 1935 - First person to fly solo nonstop from Mexico City to Newark, New Jersey; 14 hours 19 minutes;
- March, 1937 - Speed record for east-to-west flight from Oakland, California to Honolulu, Hawaii; Later crashed at Wheeler Air Force Base requiring non-design fuselage repairs;
- June 1, 1937 – Departs Miami, Florida for San Juan, Puerto Rico on the first leg of her around the world flight;
- July 1, 1937 - Departs Lae City, Papua, New Guinea airport for Howland Island;
- July 2, 1937 – Earhart and Noonan are reported missing. Their disappearance is the talk of America's July 4$^{th}$ holiday;
- July 19, 1937 – The Navy officially ends its search for Amelia;
- January 5, 1939 – The court officially declares Earhart dead;
- January, 1940 forward – "Researchers" develop four primary scenarios that take hold and are embellished through the decades. They are the Pacific Islands Theory, the Irene Bolan Theory, the down in the Ocean Theory, and the Castaways theory;
- February, 1941 - Dr. Lindsay Isaac, senior Medical Officer in charge of medical and forensic investigations, examined 13 bones forwarded from Gardener Island by Officer Gerald Gallagher. He wrote they were from an, "*elderly male of Polynesian race,*"
- April, 1941 - English Doctor David W. Hoodless M.D. (1887-1955) received the same bones in the Fiji Islands. They are old enough to have slightly disintegrated during shipment. He determined they are from a "*robust, middle-aged*" male. His, "*use of a well-established pelvic method and related femoral traits is supportive of his expertise.*"[lxxviii]
- **August, 1998** – A retired, multi-decorated, military intelligence

controlled remote viewer was tasked with Earhart's July 1, 1937 airport coordinates. His Intelligence grade map is discovered to depict the lee side of the Nikumaroro (Gardner) Atoll, in the Phoenix Island chain in the nation of Kiribati;

• 1999 to 2010 - There are repeated trips to Nikumaroro to specifically search for Castaway's Theory evidence. Each trip's theory is that Earhart's plane will be found on the land or in the lagoon. They all fail, but crash fragments are brought back. For the 2010 expedition, the TIGHAR Group reversed its ~25 year old theory stating the debris field will now be found in the ocean;

• July, 2010 - TIGHAR returns with a turtle bone claiming was a "white woman's" finger bone. The University of Oklahoma's Norman Laboratory oddly reported their findings were "inconclusive";

• March, 2012 – Secretary of State Hillary Clinton sponsors a one day Amelia Earhart symposium. For an undisclosed sum, the TIGHAR Group purchases a ten-year license agreement from the Kiribati government to prevent other Earhart exploration at Nikumaroro. A financially invested press monopoly is also involved;

• April, 2012 - Messers Gillespie, Glickman, and a camera crew fly to Rhodes House Library at Oxford University, England .to retrieve Eric Bevington's original photograph for Hillary Clinton;

• May, 2012 - Our Freedom of Information requests regarding U.S. State Department funds spent for Kiribati diplomatic travel expenses and the DOS's forensic photo analyst hours are rejected;

• July, 2012 – TIGHAR's Castaway's Theory is the basis for a failed deep water exploration off the Nikumaroro Atoll's west end;

• August, 2012 - The TIGHAR Group claims they have found an anomaly that "may be" a debris field and issue an underwater dark blue photograph with yellow arrows which are suppressed from republication. They are subsequently removed and unavailable;

• May, 2013 – An enhanced west end underwater "sound shadow" graphic, showing a silver streak at 613 feet of water, is produced by a "TIGHAR supporter" as a possible fuselage. It may have been Photo Shopped™ and is dropped;

• June, 2013 - TIGHAR's largest contributor filed a lawsuit against both the TIGHAR Group and Richard Edward Gillespie in a Casper, Wyoming Federal Court on behalf of Timothy Mellon. Mr. Mellon was represented by Jeff Oven of Crowley Fleck, PLLP of Billings, MT. and Timothy Stubson in Casper, WY. The TIGHAR

Group was represented by John Masterson of the Casper, WY law firm Rothgerber Johnson & Lyons LLP. Mr. Mellon was seeking damages of $3,140,529.00, and attorney's fees on four counts of Fraud, Negligence, Misrepresentation and Racketeering;

• August, 2013 - In U.S. District Judge Scott W. Skavdahl's Casper, WY courtroom, oral arguments took place on TIGHAR's motion to dismiss their Case# 13CV-118-S;

• September, 2013, The Judge handed down a decision allowing the lawsuit to continue, but that the racketeering and negligence charges were to be stricken;

• May, 2014 - A "Commission" established by TIGHAR confirms their sheet metal article #2-2-V-1 is not from a military aircraft;

• June, 2014 – The TIGHAR Group's 2014 trip is cancelled;

• July, 2014 - The legal case against TIGHAR is dismissed;

• May, 2015 - The Tenth Circuit U. S. Court of Appeals denied Timothy Mellon's appeal of the summary judgment concerning his law suit against the TIGHAR group;

• June, 2015 - Mr. Mellon filed a complaint with the IRS, claiming that Mr. Gillespie's high salary has no independent oversight thus violating I.R.S. nonprofit guidelines;

• June 2015 - The TIGHAR team flies to the Fiji Islands and boards the vessel *Nai'a* bound for a two-week expedition to Gardener Island. They are accompanied by a 32-cabin boutique pontoon ship, the *Fiji Princess,* filled with passengers who are there to search for evidence of castaways;

• July, 2015 - Walter Kastner, 99, of Whittier, California, dies. He was the last surviving crewman of the carrier *U.S.S. Lexington* involved with the 1937 search for Amelia Earhart;

• July, 2015 – Amid press silence, the eleventh TIGHAR Expedition returns having failed to find any evidence of castaways;

• August, 2015 – The author received a State Department packet providing "newly found" documents showing the Kiribati Foreign Minister's 2012 airfare and accommodations were paid for by the TIGHAR Group;

The author contacted the State Department requesting documents concerning TIGHAR's activities in the last week before Kiribati's Foreign Minister's arrival in the U.S. Based on conversations, he was e-mailed confirmation that the inquiry will go to someone who will get back. No return contact was made;

# Evidential Details

- July, 2017 - The History Channel™ presented a bizarre program called "*Amelia Earhart – the Lost Evidence*" using a picture to "prove" Amelia was alive after she had vanished. But historians realized their flight scenario was unworkable. Curiously, the airing was Saturday night before the Amelia Earhart Birthplace Museum Festival opened. Televised to be the topic of Festival conversation - it was. Before the festivities opened their picture was discovered in a 1935 Japanese travel book called *The Life Line of the Sea, My South Sea Memoir*. The History Channel then canceled the show's rerun withdrawing it from streaming and pay-per-view. By this book's 2020 updating, management had still failed to follow up on their promise to conduct a rigorous employee investigation!

- July, 2017 – The author met with Doctor Emeritus Richard Jantz (Forensic Biologist) in his office at the University of Tennessee, Knoxville. Their hour and 45 minute discussion focused on Earhart history and the Cross & Wright Report published in the March, 2015 *Journal of Archaeological Science*. That article analyzed two doctor's skeletal examinations on bones shipped to the Central Medical School in the Fiji Islands from Gardner Island/Nikumaroro. The *Journal's* scientific analysis concluded:

*"It is impossible to be definitive, but on balance, the most robust scientific analysis and conclusions are those of the original British finding indicating that the Nikumaroro bones belonged to a robust, middle-aged man, not Amelia Earhart."*

Analysis: In 1929 a severe storm pushed the vessel *SS Norwich City* up on to Nikumaroro's reef killing 11 unrecovered crewmen. The bones retrieved by Gerry Gallagher, in December 1940, are some of a seaman's bones that were tossed through the lagoon and landed as the waters receded. Scavenged by crabs, rodents and birds, the skeleton was picked clean with 13 bones remaining. Exposed to the hot sun, the tropical environment took its toll over the next 133 months. This accounts for why some bones crumbled during transport. Human bones would not start to disintegrate from a July, 1937 death (42 months). This time line was one of several reasons the doctors concluded the bones could not be Earhart's. The remains were of a robust sailor born ~1875-85. The crew roster should establish his name. Suffice it to say the whole european woman's body story is yet another Earhart diversion by people, with ulterior motive, who never saw the bones.

Amelia Earhart

# Section II

# *Finding Amelia*

The 1932 Distinguished Flying Cross awarded
to Amelia Earhart by the United States Congress.

*"The expedition will search for evidence
to support the* (Castaways) *theory..."*

~The TIGHAR Group~

# Evidential Details

When the Earhart mystery was first targeted we had no idea where the flight ended except that it was within fuel range of Lae City, New Guinea. When I received the map from Joseph McMoneagle, the area drawn appeared to be a reef, but in the vast South Pacific, which one? Over the next six weeks five governmental agencies and three corporations were contacted. Based on library data, and a fledgling 1990's Internet, the National Oceanic and Atmospheric Administration (NOAA) was contacted.

On October 6, 1998, Lieutenant Commander D. Cole at NOAA responded. He referred me to a Mark Friese who passed the information in many secret directions. The next morning I was referred to Captain S. Debow. A message was left.

After some telephone discussions, on October 27, Captain Debow faxed me a magazine article. Inset was a picture of the Nikumaroro Atoll's northwest corner. The search ended with that fax. The search had taken a day over six weeks.

On December 18, Captain Debow informed me NOAA would not become involved in this effort. On December 29, I had the original map dated and notarized.

Appearing in the July, 1997 edition of *GIS World Magazine*, the picture is Gardner Island, now Nikumaroro Atoll, looking east at the Nutiran Point. As low a resolution as the fax was, it was enough to recognize the land formation as the same as on the map I had received from McMoneagle.

Courtesy *Geo World Magazine*
www.geoplace.com

The *Geo World* story reported The International Group for Historic Aircraft Recovery (TIGHAR) had just returned from their "Niku III" trip. In January 1999, I called the Group's Director. During that call, he was given the debris field position. He wanted to know where I got my information. I told him about the 902nd Operation Star Gate Military Intelligence Unit. He had never heard of it, but he made it clear he was against remote viewing and that he was a supporter of the "Amazing Randi" magician de-bunker. This emerged as a worst case scenario for people that wanted the mystery solved.[13]

Around the first of October 1999, I spoke with a woman at the Amelia Earhart Birthplace Museum in Atchison, Kansas. She thought this material significant enough to provide the phone number to one of the last living persons to speak to Amelia.

During the evening of October 4, I was able to get through to Amelia Earhart's niece, Ms. Amy Kleppner, then living in Silver Spring, Maryland. A nice lady and former University Professor, we had a cordial conversation regarding the various theories about what had happened to her aunt Amelia. Later I mailed her McMoneagle's version of events and received a follow-up card with no endorsement for any particular premise.

On March 15, 2004, I spoke with Archivist Ms. Sammie Morris who was the Head, Archives and Special Collections and Associate Professor of Library Science, at the Amelia Earhart Special Digital Collections Library at Purdue University in West Lafayette, Indiana. I sent her a map to be certain a neutral party held a copy. A call was made with a fax follow-up on March, 17. Another call was placed on March, 25 to confirm receipt of the mailing and how the data would be kept.

On February 10, 2007, a Riad Kim, at the U.S. Kiribati Consulate signed for our package. The mail (return post card #7000 0520 0014 1804 8446) included my attorney's introductory letter with a map copy. According to the Hawaiian Remote Viewing Guild, the office (a private residence) was non-responsive even after a member made a house call claiming a boy answered the door. How high up the map went is unknown. But it was confirmed as signed for by the top Kiribati official in the United States in 2007.

---

[13] In a 90 minute TV show James Randi properly focused on unmasking psychic fraud and faith healers. But even though there was plenty of time remaining, he never mentioned the U.S. Intelligence and Security Command's Star Gate program.

Later that year, the National Broadcasting Company (NBC) decided to provide press coverage to the newly elected Kiribati President Anote Tong. This interview was then elevated up to an *NBC Nightly News* feature. It was goodwill press to insure continuing access to Kiribati waters.

In fairness it should be noted that many untested store front psychics have claimed to have "located" Earhart's aircraft, and all have failed. Nonetheless, as of January 1999, Mr. Gillespie was advised Amelia Earhart's airplane was in the ocean. And even though contemptuous, and refusing to look at our map, he embraced our "*in the ocean*" recommendation 12 years later at which time he wanted the world to believe it was his idea.

In the history of discovery breakthroughs generally involve questioning fundamentals. However, this is not always been the case. The President, and especially First Lady Eleanor Roosevelt, pushed government officials to solve this mystery. Nonetheless, almost ten years after Amelia's loss the various pre-Nikumaroro theories were summed up in this declassified response to an Australian military investigation into the various rumors floating around the Pacific.

 # U.S. Department of Justice

April 16, 1947

**To:** Lt. Colonel Longfield Lloyd, Commonwealth Investigative Branch, Canberra, A.C.T. (Australian Capital Territory)

*As you might have surmised, we have in the past received many communications suggesting that Mrs. Putnam is still alive. None of these has been found to have any foundation in fact...*

*I regret I cannot be of further assistance to you in this matter.*

J. Edgar Hoover,
Director
Federal Bureau of Investigation[lxxix]

Amelia Earhart

# The Atoll's Enigma

The Kiribati National Flag

Kiribati's Location

The Nikumaroro Atoll, known as Gardner Island for about 150 years, has been safe place for Fred and Amelia to hide. The island is in the Kiribati Republic (pronounced keer-ah-bhass) which gained independence from the United Kingdom in July, 1997. Micronesian, Kiribati is on the equator approximately half way between Australia and Hawaii. Its capital is Tarawa. Its currency is the Australian dollar. Per capita income was US$ 3,350 in 2019.

Data SIO, NOAA, U.S. Navy, NGA, GEBCO, Image NASA 2009
The Nikumaroro Atoll - looking down into an extinct volcanic caldera (lagoon). The TIGHAR Group says Earhart landed electrically intact (upper left) and broadcast a contested number of messages for 5-6 days. In 2012, they locked out all research with their ten year Kiribati Government Antiquities Licensing Agreement.

At approximately 180 miles south of the equator, Kiribati's primary island groups are the Line, Phoenix and Gilbert chains. Nikumaroro is in the Phoenix Group. The nation's total sovereign expanse is close to the continental United States. But their land mass consists of 33 coral atoll's of 266 square miles (811km$^2$) making it about four times the size of the District of Columbia.

On September 20, 1979 representatives of the Republic of Kiribati and the United States met in Tarawa to sign a friendship treaty known as the Treaty of Tarawa, which recognized Kiribati sovereignty. The U.S. Senate approved the accord on June 21,

1983, to be effective on September 23 with an exchange of ratification instruments at Suva, Fiji. During this period the atoll's name was changed from Gardner to Nikumaroro.

Due to its larger size, multi-national inspections and lengthy colonization during the 20th century, the Gardener/Nikumaroro Island has a comparatively richer history. Because one of those expeditions should have encountered evidence of TIGHAR's castaways, we review events to help the historian decide if adequate third party inspections have taken place. These events are in chronological order.

U.S. Navy Photo
Assigned to inspect M'Kean and Gardner Islands, at 7 a.m. Friday July 9, Corsair Vought 030 bi-planes (center left) were catapulted from the *U.S.S. Colorado's* stern.

**1)** One week after Earhart's disappearance, a U.S. Navy spotter plane flew over Nikumaroro. After the flight, the *USS Colorado's* senior aviator, Lieutenant John Lambrecht, reported:

*From M'Kean (Atoll) the planes proceeded to Gardner Island (sighting the [USS Colorado] ship to starboard enroute) and made an aerial search of this island which proved to be one of the biggest of the {Phoenix] group.*

*Here signs of recent habitation were clearly visible but repeated circling and zooming failed to elicit any answering wave from possible inhabitants and it was finally taken for granted that none were there.*[lxxx]

If Earhart was really castaway, why was there no signaling for help? What Earhart had onboard is unconfirmed. But when she attempted to take off in Hawaii in March, the airplane carried: powerful two-cell Eveready flashlights with batteries; a signal pistol with a 14" signal pistol shell; parachute flares; a box kite and Bausch & Lomb field glasses with carrying case.

U.S. Navy Photo

At about 450 feet (137m) a week after Earhart's disappearance. Circling for 15 minutes, the aviators were low enough to see people waiving clothing during low tide.

**2)** On October 13, 1937, British Lands Commissioner Henry E. Maude visited Gardner Island (Nikumaroro) with Cadet Officer Eric Bevington and 19 Gilbertese.

*Western Pacific High Commission*
*Cadet Officer Eric R. Bevington*

They walked the atoll and found no evidence of castaways, or airplane debris. According to the officer: "*The island was thoroughly explored from end to end.*" and that, "*Maude's lumbago was bad, so I* (Bevington) *was to take the Gilbertese round the island, walking so we could see everything of it.*"[lxxxi] They found nothing when theoretically 100 days later Earhart or Noonan could have still been alive with the island's, coconuts, large crab and, "*sheltered lagoon with plentiful fish.*"[lxxxii]

**3)** On December 1, 1938 the New Zealand cruiser *HMS Leander* landed with its Pacific Aviation Expeditioners who surveyed Gardner Island as a seaplane/airfield destination. Over the weeks, they buoyed Nikumaroro's channels and coral heads with 55-gallon drums. They found no evidence of castaways.

Royal New Zealand Air Force

The New Zealand Air Force Survey Team. They are in front of their latest design seaplane, "Supermarine Walrus I", from which pictures of Nikumaroro were taken.

In June 2013, the Royal New Zealand Air Force Museum photograph archiver, in Christchurch, N.Z. - Matthew O'Sullivan - discovered six unmarked photos of Gardner Island. They were taken during this twelve man expedition. While interesting, the photos shed no new light on the Earhart mystery.

**4)** On December 20, 1938 a Gilbert Islanders work party was brought to Gardner to begin clearing a village site. The original colony population was 58 including 16 women and 26 children. But no remains or evidence of castaways were found by the settlers just 18 months after Earhart's disappearance.

**5)** During November and December 1939, men of the *USS Bushnell* landed and roamed the terrain. They surveyed and mapped the island while taking astronomical observations. They found no evidence of castaways.

United States Navy picture #102-1
The 1918 *USS Bushnell* with World War I submarines alongside (lower right).

**6)** In September, 1940 British Colonial Officer Gerald B. Gallagher established a *Phoenix Island Settlement Scheme* Headquarters on Gardner Island. What is pertinent is his correspondence with British Secretary of the Western Pacific High Commission in Suva, Fiji, Sir Henry Harrison Vaskess (1891-1969, retired 1948).

On September 23, Gerry Gallagher reported some unusual objects on the island's southeast end. His itemization included an empty <u>sextant box</u> and a <u>sextant's inverting eyepiece</u> along with a shoe heel and some human bones. With Earhart in mind, on October 6, Gallagher wrote the Administrative Officer, Central Gilbert Islands District, Tarawa that the, *"Possibility of this being Mrs. Putnam is naturally remote"*. An unfortunate editorial+.

On October 17, Gallagher also reported to Secretary Vaskess that: "*Bones were found on South East corner of* (the) *island about 100 feet above ordinary high water springs.*" His 100 foot remark is interpreted to mean 33 yards (30.5m) inland from the high tide vegetation line. He also reported he had searched the area, indicating a thoroughly organized search would take weeks. Also aware of the Earhart mystery, on October 26 Commissioner Vaskess instructed Gallagher to undertake an, *"organized search."*

In his December 27 Quarterly Report, Gallagher confirmed that bones and artifacts had been packaged for shipment to the Suva, Fiji Islands Medical School.

Clearly, a sextant box and a technologically advanced inverting eyepiece suggests navigation. Based on McMoneagle's map, this is the correct place for Noonan's sextant equipment. As cockpit items blew through the windshield onto the reef, they would have moved obliquely to an uncertain degree with the vagaries of surf, wind and tidal advances.

Gerald Bernard Gallagher (1912 - 1941) Gardener Island's Chief Colonial Officer. He, "*Was a fine and promising young officer whose enthusiasm and devoted leadership proved of prime importance.*"

But there are real problems with a corpse washing 100 feet into the jungle. With a waterborne ditching, their safety harnesses would have been secured. Remember, when they hit the coral:

**McMoneagle - Both passengers are unconscious, bleeding from facial and head wounds. The plane fills with water in what appears to be half a minute or less and sinks quickly below the waves.**

In 1991, the TIGHAR Group found a brass shoelace eyelet, a shoe heel, and a ripped sole they claim to have been Earhart's which automatically proved their Castaways Theory! While we neither accept nor deny their authenticity, footwear destroyed to this degree supports a ripping and tearing scenario.

While enroute to the Fiji Islands, in February, 1941, on the R.C.S. *Nimanoa* a Dr. Linsay Isaac examined the bones and wrote they were from an, "*elderly male of Polynesian race,*" adding, "*the bones have been in sheltered position for upwards of 20 years and possibly much longer.*" (Isaac, 1941b)[lxxxiii]

Secondly, upon examination at the Fiji Medical Center that April, Dr. D.W. Hoodless independently determined the remains most likely belonged to a 5' 5 1/2" stocky male of European or mixed European ancestry, probably between 45–55 years old. Neither doctor had spoken or corresponded with each other.

Upon receipt of the Hoodless report, Central Medical Authority Dr. Duncan C.M. MacPherson MB ChB (1900-1943) concluded that the remains were not those of Amelia Earhart and the case was closed with no further action taken on an unknown male.

Commissioner Vaskess' note to England was found in file 4439-40, dated April 11, 1941. Transcript: "His Excellency, *The Report 11 appears to definitely indicate that the skeleton cannot be that of the late Amelia Earhart, but Y. E.* [Your Excellency] *may wish action taken as suggested in paragraph 9 of 11 although it does not seem possible that any useful purpose will be served by proceeding farther.*"

Gerry Gallagher had found bones and artifacts but no indication of castaways. He died at Gardner Island on September 24, 1941 apparently from food poisoning. We honor his service by calling the atoll's southeastern end the *Gallagher Curvature.*

With the December 7, 1941 Japanese attack on Pearl Harbor, Hawaii, war swept the South Pacific. Accordingly, on July 21, 1942, British Major General Sir Philip Mitchell, (KCMG, MC) was sent to be the Military Governor of the Fiji Islands.

*Major General Sir Philip Euen Mitchell (1890-1964). With Governor Vaskess reassigned, his dismissive correspondence to higher authority, Gerry Gallagher dead, and the Japanese on the move toward the Fiji Islands, Mitchell's command is the most likely to have presided over what happened to the artifacts received from Gardener Island.*

Richard Frost

The Islands were readied for defense, as they were the forward airfields the Japanese needed to strike New Zealand. "*No useful purpose*" emerged as the rationale to dispose of Gallagher's items. One account states the bones were shipped to Australia but no import entry has been unearthed. Once the military threat was gone, Mitchell was reassigned to Kenya in December, 1944.

7) In June 1944, less than seven years after Earhart's disappearance, a U.S. Navy survey took place at Gardner Island to deter-

mine if it would be a good place to establish a Long Range Aid to Navigation (Loran) Station at 4 41 41.65S - 174 29 50.61W. Land clearance started on July 24.

Courtesy Steve Sopko, son of Commanding Officer Charles Sopko (lower center with hat)
Men of the 1944 U.S. Coast Guard Loran Unit 92, Gardner Island, South Pacific.

Construction began on September 1, and the first radio tests went out on September 20. The Loran station was commissioned on December 16, with a 25-man crew. "While manned, the Americans made great friends with the settlers. Time had been found to build sailing canoes. On the sheltered waters of Nikumaroro lagoon these could be fine, swift racing craft and the visitors learned the unrivalled thrill of racing these twenty-knot, knife-edge fliers."[lxxxiv]

In May, 1946, U.S. Loran operations ceased following the end of World War II in August, 1945. The men had roamed the island for 20 months without any discovery of castaway's items.

8) During this period, navy pilot John Mims (later an M.D. in Alabama) flew seaplane mail and supply flights from Kanton Island into Gardner's lagoon. One day he noticed some villagers using a steel cable for a fishing line leader. When he asked where they got it, the natives told him it was from the "*crashed airplane.*" Torn from the port wing, debris like aileron cable whiplashed over the reef, which tends to confirm the colonists crashed airplane statement.

**McMoneagle - Get a sense the left engine separated with a section of wing and drove itself into the coral bank, tearing the port side of the plane apart.**

Also, during a heavy weather stop at Funafuti, Tuvalu during TIGHAR's Niku III expedition (Feb. 20 - Mar. 22, 1997), former Nikumaroro colonists were interviewed. *"While there, they documented two eye-witness accounts of aircraft wreckage seen on the island's shoreline in the late 1950s."*[lxxxv] But there was no reference to which shoreline. If found on the southeast end Mr. Gillespie has had the keys to the mystery since 1997, but still asserted his particularized Castaways Theory.

Those interviews put three eyewitnesses on the aircraft wreckage record, with no sightings of safely landed castaways from anyone, anywhere, anytime.

**9)** In September 1947, British Chief Lands Commissioner, B.C. Cartland performed an Phoenix Islands Group inspection spending three days on Nikumaroro. Nothing of castaways was reported.

**10)** On January 1, 1949, an unnamed Lands Commissioner from Mr. Cartland's staff arrived and spent days at Nikumaroro. He oversaw the establishment of family residential sites on the island. During this process no evidence of castaways was found.

**11)** Paul B. Laxton, the Western Pacific High Commission's District Officer for the Phoenix Group during and after World War II, stayed at Nikumaroro for three months reorganizing the colony. He made no mention of castaways.

During the mid-1950s, the atoll's population reached approximately 100 people. By the early 1960s, the colony became unsustainable due to the lack of fresh water in a drought requiring ongoing supply. In 1963 the British moved the residents to the Solomon Islands. Rationalists insist some Castaways evidence should have been discovered during the colonist's 13 years there.

**12)** In 1978, Kiribati authorities conducted a sovereignty survey of the island during their transition to nationhood and found no evidence of castaways.

It was preparatory to the 2010 trip (May 18 - June 14) that TIGHAR's web site conceded they would search for Earhart's debris field in the ocean. But they failed to explain how the wave action that, for 25 years, pushed the plane onto land or into the lagoon, could now move the same plane in the opposite direction. But, this 180 degree premise reversal did move them closer to the debris field, and our 1998 *"hocus pocus"* conclusion. After 20 years later their *"on the land or in the lagoon"* hypothesis was completely discarded providing insight into TIGHAR's scientific ramp.

After we pointed out the tides were too high for the propellers to turn during some of their daily 100 "genuine" messages, a corrected count was required. So they quietly eliminated the messages sent during high tides from the original count.[14]

TIGHAR rejects 12 competent individuals or groups who, reporting to four different governments for over 40 years (1937-1978), encountered no castaway's evidence. Add 11 specifically targeted, high technology, TIGHAR expeditions (1989-2015), and you are in position to assess these 23 castaways let downs.

Add all this to the fact that in 1929, the shipwrecked *S.S. Norwich City* radioed an SOS, were heard, and rescued. But according to the Castaways Theory, Fred and Amelia broadcast for five or six days to a specifically tasked, higher military technology, 24 hour airwave monitoring, aircraft carrier task force, and not one Earhart voice message got through. So TIGHAR is forced to honor those bad aircraft antenna messages heard in the United States all the way to Florida as genuine because the listener said so. And to be the last person to hear Amelia's voice would make that person an Earhart V.I.P.

As it turned out, the TIGHAR Group painted themselves into the atoll's northwest corner and then became contradictory:

TIGHAR: *"We considered the primary search area to be the reef slope between the Bevington Object and the wreck of SS Norwich City."*[lxxxvi]

But the highest point on the west end is north of the Bevington object. Holding to the dry transmitter requirement during a week of high tides, the search would have been from the Bevington Object to the northwest corner – not south of the "object."

In the July, 2012 search, no aircraft debris was found. But something was needed to sustain this tax free "non-profit." So the U.S. media now presented "data" that obscured the trip's true

---

[14] Notably, it was not until after the 2012 trip that Mr. Gillespie posted a high tide inquiry on TIGHAR's Internet Forum (November 28, 2012). Quote: *"This thread is for discussions of the probable height above ground of the propeller tips of Earhart's Electra when it was parked on a flat surface."* This determination was critical to electrical generation before publishing their high tide "credible" messages count.

implications.[15]

The public was to believe those *"tantalizing clues"* that *"hint"* at the Castaways theory were true. But publishing that smashed, *"Jars hint at Amelia Earhart as a Castaway"* was untrue. Smashed glass indicates an impact or smashing event.

Re-enter photo analyst Jeff Glickman. As he reviewed the trip's underwater videos, he said there might be strange shapes on the western end of the atoll; and uncertainty was the key to gifts.

So, on or about August 20, 2012, TIGHAR announced Earhart's plane *"appeared"* to be found; that dark objects, *"might ...resemble"* something like a plane wreck. A dark blue underwater graphic with yellow arrows pointing to the "debris" was displayed with the following statement:

## *Earhart Debris Field Found*

*A review of high-definition underwater video footage taken during the recently completed Niku VII expedition has revealed a scattering of manmade objects on the reef slope off the west end of Nikumaroro. The newly discovered debris field is in deep water offshore the location where an object <u>thought to be</u> a Lockheed Electra landing gear appears in a photo taken three months after Amelia Earhart disappeared. Items in the debris field <u>appear to be</u> consistent with the object in the 1937 photo.*

It was all wrong. These objects were falsely referred to as *"manmade"* which is terminology entry level remote viewing students use when working pictograms! However, once lightened up, these images did not show a debris field and Mr. Glickman clarified by saying the whole thing had been *strictly preliminary*.

Nevertheless, for the faithful a phony headline was all that was needed to put a waft back into their Castaways sails. Unfortunately, their use of copyright law as a sword rather than a shield keeps us from bringing you these images. So as they *"reparse,"* the public became aware of the decided need for third party verification on any TIGHAR Earhart find.

---

[15] For fiscal (June) 2013-2014, *"Principal Officer"* Richard Gillespie filed IRS Form 990 showing his salary at $185,623 over and above their $461,467 spent for *"Total Functional Expense"* providing, *"ongoing investigation...including field work, analysis, research and <u>writing</u>, to promote responsible aviation archaelogy..."* This included member services, fund raising, spousal rent and general administration reimbursements as approved by TIGHAR's *"independent"* Board of Directors.

Another issue became the TIGHAR named Seven Site located in the island's <u>North Aukaraime</u> sector. On May 30, 2012, a *Discovery Communications*™ editorial, come news report, referenced the Seven Site as: *"on the <u>southeast end</u> of Nikumaroro Island ...a partial skeleton of a castaway* (see Doctors. Isaac & Hoodless p. 90) *was discovered at the so called seven site in 1940..."*

Hold on. Maps show the Seven Site on the <u>Northside</u>! The southeast end is where McMoneagle's map indicated to search 14 years earlier. So what was the motive for this fake news location?

Then on May 28, 2013, as first reported by the *Discovery Channel*, a brand new, *sound based* fuselage image was trotted out that we would love to provide. The image looked like a sideways liquid mercury streak from an iodine dropper. Once again, we have before and after graphics showing a substantial silver color enhancement of their *"anomaly."* Photo Shopped? Later that year, when referring to this same graphic, Mr. Gillespie told CNN Hong Kong: *Yeah, I'd call it a big break through.*

But this sound based imagery also fizzled resulting in a return to their *"laying old theories to rest"* habit. So TIGHAR's next potential step was to rule out our data by moving around to the atoll's southeast end. But this trail was blazed in 2012, using a multibeam underwater sonar bathymetric mapping system onboard the University of Hawaii research vessel operated by PhD's from the Hawaiian Underwater Research Laboratory (HURL).

The most significant development of TIGHAR's 2012 expedition was the first time ocean floor mapping of the atoll's southeast end. A ridge was discovered in approximately 650 feet (198m) of water. This previously unknown roll obstruction was exactly where, and at the depth, Mr. McMoneagle's 1998 data indicated (p. 78). And this time we were stopped from bringing you a University vessel generated image by a contract technicality.

TIGHAR's next expedition took place in 2015. After a five day, thousand mile voyage from the Fiji islands, TIGHAR's vessel *Nai'a*, arrived at Nikumaroro on June 13.

On a separate, 55 meter (180ft), dual hulled, boutique liner called the *Fiji Princess*, 61 "tourists" also sailed to Nikumaroro, anchoring in the atoll's southern waters. Castaways research was to be conducted on the smaller *Nai'a* vessel on the west end.

Our correspondence with Blue Lagoon Cruises indicated the *Fiji Princess's* corporate sonar only goes down 60 meters, which could not have detected Earhart's debris field. But, was this the only metal detector onboard? TIGHAR's silent partners are fully aware of McMoneagle's capabilities. So, the introduction of a two boat strategy emerged as the perfect maneuver. Every prospect existed for a southeast end magnetometer trolling to have been conducted. And with the coordinated press silence surrounding the 2015 journey, they re-emphased their 1991 ripped and cracked fuselage skin reviewed on pages 81-82.

If TIGHAR located the debris field with the dual ship maneuver it may represent a break that is in the public interest. At this point we move on to one of the *Castaways* major cornerstones.

# TIGHAR's Earhart Messages Reviewed

Earhart's radio "*messages*" is indispensable to the Castaway's grip. But if landed safely, how much broadcast and listening time would the airplane's batteries provide? How much fuel was required to run the starboard engine for 5-6 days?

Throughout the Twentieth Century, TIGHAR's web site avowed that half of 200 distress signals *"seem to have been genuine"* meaning Fred and Amelia were alive. Experts are uncertain, but using their original number, the airtime to send their original *"genuine messages"* was about 415 minutes, or close to seven hours. And those numbers do not include listening time. Adequate fuel reserves have always been a TIGHAR unmentionable given! So we decided to review every message to confirm how they were classified. We published our findings in 2012.

With that, their claim was blown wide open. The TIGHAR Group immediately revised their *"working hypothesis"* downward. Their new numbers specified that only **57 out of 100** messages were now genuinely Earhart. Reduced by half, this represented a **43% reduction** in credible Earhart/Noonan transmissions.

So, because of their significance, loyal TIGHAR member Bob Brandenburg, PhD., worked a third set of numbers.[16] These figures were broken down into a messages per day format.

July 3 = **14**: July 4 = **13**: July 5 = **24**: July 6 = **5** [lxxxvii]

---

[16] Bob Brandenburg's revised "signal catalog" used criterion like radio reception only on 3105 kHz or 6210 kHz. However, he also included harmonics and other "*positive qualitative factors.*" Like what?

Dr. Brandenburg declared there were 56 true Earhart messages out of his now upwardly mobile 182 total. But, he also eliminated all the July 7 messages, providing an extra 24 hours for Amelia's airplane to be washed into the sea before Navy pilots arrived. Apparently, this "washed into the sea" lead time would look more plausible if extended from 38 to 62 hours from her last transmission. But no one bought it.

TIGHAR's fourth accounting was unearthed in an August 5, 2016 speech at a Collider Meeting at the Beer City Science Pub in Ashville, North Carolina. Apparently unconvinced, Mr. Gillespie reasserted the July 7 transmission scenario, but now the total message count was 120 (down from Dr. Brandenburg's 182) of which the original **57 credible messages were re-affirmed**.

Then there were five. Mr. Gillespie quote: "*Earhart made a relatively safe landing at Gardner Island and sent radio distress calls for six days,*" reaffirmed his six-day scenario. Then Mr. Gillespie said in a YouTube presentation. "*There are 47 mes-sages heard by professional radio operators that <u>appear</u> to be credible.*"[lxxxviii] This new **47 credible messages** was down by ten

Malleable. TIGHAR Group member/researcher Dr. Gary LaPook conducted an analysis whose (correct) conclusion was that the tides around Nikumaroro were not deep enough to pull an Electra 10 over the edge during this time period. Nor were the waters rough enough to break off the Electra's crash re-engineered landing strut. Remember, this is a cornerstone in their foundation.

**Analysis:** Unbelievably, none of these "messages" referred to a rescue coordinate which is the whole purpose of S.O.S. communi-cations. It is well known the plane's propellers could not spin without being in the air or on its landing gear. In addition, idling, the right engine at the normal 700 rpm would not produce adequate transmitter power from the plane's "undersized" generator.

The two Bendix-Eclipse 50-ampere generators, powered by the right engine, supplied electricity for the Western Electric radio whose popped connection cable was recovered at Niku-maroro. Both 85 ampere batteries might supply power for 90 minutes, but once drained, could not crank the engine the next day. Earhart's radio time hinged on re-charging and that required six day fuel reserves that no one but TIGHAR believes existed, and McMoneagle reported as exhausted (p. 76). Because this large fuel supply cannot be confirmed, it is sheer assumption.

# Evidential Details

By the summer of 1937, almost every inhabited island in Micronesia, Melanesia, and Polynesia had radio. TIGHAR's use of terms like, *plausible; suggests; apparently; or appears to be,* were routinely used to categorize messages as credible. However, all this was subsequently unmasked as primarily telegraph key with some normal South Pacific radio chatter. Therefore, it made sense when TIGHAR's Senior Archaeologist Tom King confirmed: "*One of the problems was that neither Earhart nor Noonan were proficient with Morse Code.*" Other historians state flatly neither one knew Morse. And radio wave direction finding equipment was in its early stages. Under no circumstances would we use this type of "substantiation" in the Evidential Details Mystery Series.

Still led by Mr. Gillespie's Castaway's Theory, TIGHAR's ocean efforts remained off the island's west end. This reef shelf theoretically could have been used as a wet tidal runway, but only along the coral shelf's closest 50 yards to the sea. Slightly tilted seaward, this slick fills with water first and provides a tighter landing window by empting last.

Vague on this detail, their hypothesis is that Amelia found the only part of the atoll where she could land <u>electrically intact</u> precisely when the reef edge was tide free. Then, with no geographic or tidal information, she taxied to the highest part of the atoll. At 34" off the ground, the transmitter needed protection from being touched by a 76" salt water high tide. As new lines of questions emerged, TIGHAR referred inquiries to their "research" articles.[17]

Another course change was TIGHAR's acceptance of our blown off course in cloudy skies scenario. Originally, they insisted Earhart was flying in spotty sun north and south on the 157-337 longitude and "*just wound up*" 400 miles off course approaching Nikumaroro from the north. But this means Fred Noonan could not determine if he was north or south of equator! Amazingly TIGHAR members look the other way on what is, by all accounts, another unreasoned supposition.

---

[17] "TIGHAR science" builds on Castaway "research." This may contain a combination of algebraic formulae, PhD level jargon, and Greenwich Mean Time vs. Pacific Time Zones interchangeability. All support the Castaway's Theory. It discourages the public, and sponsors, from challenging their conclusions by leaving the impression all relevant questions have been answered, and that a substantial learning curve is required for any meaningful participation.

At the July, 2011 Amelia Earhart Birthplace Museum Festival Mr. Gillespie appeared for the only time. Here we met and were cordial throughout the day. Later, I e-mailed TIGHAR for permission to use a picture from their web site.

<u>Ric Gillespie</u>: *"You do not have and we will not grant you permission to use...* <u>*any*</u> *of the images from the TIGHAR website. If you use them we will sue you."*

So, TIGHAR's membership contributes to the first "scientific non-profit," in world history to threaten to sue a "psychic book" author over visual aids intended to enhance public understanding.

The July 2017, History Channel™ picture used to <u>prove</u> Earhart was still alive after July, 1937. But the picture was found in a 1935 Japanese library book and the multi-million dollar farce was quickly dropped. Amelia Earhart was never in Saipan.

# Third Party Validators

**1.) That our map location was tentative:**
- Geographic location established through the National Oceanographic and Atmospheric Administration N.O.A.A.) Ship's Captain. Additionally, nine geographic points were identified between our map and satellite imagery (p. 77);

**2.) That windshield Plexiglas™ parts are not from an Electra:**
- Confirmed as a Lockheed Electra 10 replacement part by the U.S. National Transportation Safety Board [NTSB] (p. 80);

**3.) That the aluminum fuselage skin found at Nikumaroro is not from an Electra 10;**
- Its use and rivet spacings confirmed by Restoration Division Staff at the U.S. Air Force National Museum at Wright-Patterson AFB in Ohio (p. 81-82);

**4.) That Nikumaroro/Gardener Island's tidal data was in sync with Mr. McMoneagle's arrival timing:**
- Confirmed by the United Kingdom's Hydrographic Office Easy Tide™ database;

**5.) That an ocean floor ridge, off Nikumaroro's southeast end, obstructing a fuselage roll, exists as we indicated in 1998:**
- Confirmed in July, 2012 when PhD's, at the Hawaiian Underwater Research Laboratory (University of Hawaii), first mapped the Island's southeast end's ocean floor;

**6.) That our reef drawings showed structures 14 years before their discovery:**
- Confirmed via Google Earth 3D satellite imagery (p. 66-67);

**7.) That the Electra's rear belly antenna mast problems existed upon Earhart's Lae City runway departure:**
- Confirmed in a forensic photo analysis of Amelia Earhart's 1937 Lae City Airport take off movie (p. 59).

Amelia Earhart

# Theater

# Rain

U.S. Secretary of State Hillary Clinton's
Amelia Earhart State Department Reception.

*"I especially want to welcome Tessie Lambourne, the Secretary for
Foreign Affairs and Immigration of the Republic of Kiribati. I also want to
acknowledge Ric Gillespie of the International Group for Historical Aircraft
Recovery."* (TIGHAR)

# Evidential Details

On March 20, 2012, seventy-five years to the day of Amelia's crash at Wheeler Air base in Hawaii, U.S. Secretary of State Hillary Clinton used America's State Department facilities to promote a private business arrangement. For this ceremonial, she introduced then Secretary of Transportation Ray LaHood, Kiribati Diplomatic Representative Tessie Lambourne, Dr. Robert Ballard of Woods Hole Oceanographic, and Richard Gillespie, to announce TIGHAR's financially strapped 75th Anniversary Earhart expedition to the International Press Corp.

In an attempt to cover-up the U.S. Government's involvement in a <u>strictly</u> commercial affair, a suspicious ad hoc Pacific Nations Friendship Initiative was announced that did nothing to update U.S. Pacific Rim policy. So the facade was that this would help counter Chinese regional hegemony which had been severely neglected during Clinton's tenure. Declaring her upcoming resignation (January, 2013), she wanted to proclaim Earhart's discovery on her watch whilst helping TIGHAR's sponsors recoup their unproductive charitable contributions.

As was pre-arranged, the Kiribatis' would sign an Antiquities Management Agreement licensing the TIGHAR Group exclusive rights to search, study, recover and preserve objects *anywhere within the territorial boundaries* of the Republic of Kiribati that even suggested the presence of an airplane. The language was wide open, the license for ten years - the price secret.

Reacting to this book, for the next decade: *"No one is authorized to undertake Earhart related search, recovery of artifacts or research within the boundaries of Kiribati without authorization from both the government of Kiribati and TIGHAR."*

Even worse for Earhart research, the TIGHAR licensing process is subjective. As Mr. Gillespie warns about withholding his *"endorsement"*, his *"grant"* language is condescending. He wants to review your credentials, your technology, your logistics, your whole plan and admonishes he will be with you every step of the way. Then, if you don't pay his indeterminate price, he has the right to deny your application and usurp your plan. This autocratic encumbrance hangs over the mystery until at least March, 2022.

Upon this announcement, TIGHAR's webmaster wiped their Nikumaroro southeast end (South Aukaraime) web page. Sadly, our screen shot cannot be provided here due to infringement threats. Destroying web site data is considered speech!

TIGHAR's second ace is the exclusive reporting rights of a financially conflicted press pipe. Implicit in TIGHAR's fiefdom is a gag order. Currently only one press concern is permitted into this part of the planet. All other media provide the story second hand.

U.S. Department of State

The FBI statement to Congress was that she, "*frequently and blatantly* *disregarded* *protocol.*" Hillary Clinton's four year $100+ million private Foundation building State Department stint was a consolation prize for losing the 2008 Democratic primary to Barak Obama. Her single action lasting ten-years took place on March 20, 2012 in the State Department's Benjamin Franklin Room. Here she sponsored a Nikuma-roro Atoll lockdown pact to support TIGHAR's supporters. Included were (seated left to right) Secretary of Transportation Ray LaHood, TIGHAR's Ric Gillespie and Dr. Robert Ballard of Woods Hole Oceanographic. Using the U.S. Navy's premier deep-sea contractor, TIGHAR's expedition failed 120 days later.

Their monopoly was summed up in this way:

> "*Sorry, but we have an exclusive arrangement*
> *under contract with Discovery Communications.*"
> ~TIGHAR~

This 75th Anniversary trip was initiated with the reintro-duction of Eric Bevington's 1937 Nikumaroro reef picture. Fraud-ulently reporting the picture's left side had been cropped, the ploy was that TIGHAR had never seen the entire picture! This became even more curious when State Department personnel advised me by phone they were not allowed to comment on this photo business because it was being handled at the highest levels.

Still undisclosed is who paid for the debt ridden TIGHAR Groups' Messers Gillespie, Glickman, and camera crew to fly to Rhodes House Library at Oxford University, England? On April 28, 2012, they shot a quality video about retrieving Bevington's original photograph. But a maximum resolution scan could have been uploaded via the Internet or couriered to the States. Either way, Secretary Clinton ordered it into State's Photo Analyst Bureau's workload for analysis and reporting.

Taxpayer dollars paid State Department salaries, pension and benefit packages to help TIGHAR's sponsors. Without those still classified federal analyst hours, the 2012 expedition might not have had the pretext to solicit additional contributions.

Originally it appeared TIGHAR had contacted the State Department for support. But, in what was absolutely unprecedented, State reached out to become involved in TIGHAR's commercial affairs. In a speech, Mr. Gillespie summed up how it worked:

*"When I had an offer of some help from the State Department, I said sure. If we can have a skilled photo analysts from the State Department take a look at this photo, we will see if there is anything to this. And they did and they gave us the results and (as was pre-arranged) they said, 'You know, we think you're right.'"*

It was Hillary Clinton approaching to help TIGHAR's sponsors. And of course, they were under no obligation to mention the competition to a federal officer when receiving diplomatic endorsements. Not surprisingly, naming the individuals that foisted the Antiquities Management Agreement into the State Department is one of this mystery's deepest darkest secrets.

So TIGHAR's website proclaimed: *"Photo analysts at the U.S. State Department's Bureau of Intelligence and Research"*, invested a highly classified amount of time on this "new" graphic. The picture was then presented to the Secretary of State who magnanimously donated her time and the federal facilities. In an interview, TIGHAR's Senior Archaeologist, Tom King said:

*"So, that all led to a Press Conference at the State Department a few months ago which Hillary Clinton gave a talk and encouraged support for an expedition to go seek the wreck of the Electra."*

Elsewhere in the Internet news, the <u>LATimes.com</u> wrote:

"*The State Department has <u>helped clear the way</u> for the expedition since the island is now part of the Republic of Kiribati.*"

On the <u>WebProNews</u> *Science Page,* June 12, 2012:

*Photographic analysts from the US State Department believe there is a significant chance that this is the wreckage of Amelia Earhart's final flight.[lxxxix]*

What was so deceitful about this picture "discovery" was that years earlier TIGHAR's internet forum had openly speculated about their new object in the "cropped" area. And their Archaeologist referred to it years earlier in this book's first edition review!

At this point it is important to state the author has nothing against the Federal Government. There are however reservations about historically acknowledged unethical tenure. So the question remains, how many tax dollars were spent on planning, visa clearances, banquet room prep, janitorial, photo-analyst hours, departmental communications, and the Secretary of State's presentation time for the Castaways Theory? We wanted to get it right. So we contacted the State Department on March 26, 2012 and spoke with a Darragh Paradiso who said there was no government "role" with the Earhart investigation.

Incredulous, I called back to talk with intake. I was told to file a Freedom of Information Act Inquiry. Two were filed. One for the Kiribati Representatives Trans-Pacific trip expenses, and one for State Department photo analyst hours

Shortly thereafter, I received a brush off e-mail from the watchful Mr. Paradiso. He turned out to be the Director, Office of Public Affairs, Bureau of East Asian and Pacific Affairs. He monitored inquiries on this Earhart business. He wrote:

*In our earlier phone conversation, I addressed a number of the questions you just sent my colleagues when I explained that the Department of State does not have an <u>active role in TIGHAR's search</u>,* (**True**) *and that <u>no taxpayer money</u> is being spent on this project.* (**False**)

The TIGHAR Group had stated flatly on their web site that the reason to obtain the Bevington photograph was so it could be reviewed by State Department photo-analysts. The need for an original was a first step to protect the Secretary from a scam. So we have created a quick little time line to show how concerned the Clinton team was about their Earhart spectacular.

**State: March 29**, 2012 Subject: FOIA receipt of Request Letter confirmed – the research process will begin?

**State: April 27**, 2012 Stated our inquiry was transferred to Office of Information Programs and Services; Case# assigned;

**People:** May 17, 2012 *What is the average amount of time a response should take?*

**State**: May 18, 2012 (next day) Stated the average time for FOIA requests is between 5 and 10 months;

**People:** May 19, 2012 Requested procedure for speeding up the FOIA process;

**State:** May 19, 2012 The State Department's e-mail address was now blocked. *"Delivery failed 3 attempts: FOIAStatus@state.gov."*

This confirmed they decided to be non-transparent on this inquiry. With the cessation of e-mail came the brush off letters.

**June 4, 2012** (2.5 months) A Department of State (DOS) hand typed letter explained why they would not respond to the inquiry about employee time used in TIGHAR's picture analysis. *"You have not reasonably described the records you seek in a way that someone familiar with Department records and programs could locate them,"* which would never have been sent to Hillary Clinton issuing the same inquiry. We were subsequently told by phone you cannot use the word TIGHAR in an inquiry even though they were the information's recipient! A phony red tape technicality.

**August 21, 2012** The "Chief Requester" wrote to now solicit money on our free file indicating they would write again, when, *"responsive material has been retrieved and reviewed."*

**August 27, 2012** A phone call to the State Department indicated our file was closed the same day as the June 4 mailing. So it made no sense that they should even follow-up on August 21.

Then I received an unusual hand written (computer dodging) letter. After almost 80 days it stated we were now reversed from *in the queue* to their *not reasonably described* catch-all language. Told to start over, we resubmitted the request for the Kiribati Representative and her husband's, travel expenses. Suddenly there was a change in the Staff's telephone demeanor. Again they asked for money to look up free information. What developed seemed very much akin to obstruction until we received another letter advising us to wait longer on this "closed" file!

Subsequent correspondence stated, "*It is the Department's policy to treat each request for a fee waiver on a case-by-case basis. ...your request for a fee waiver has* (naturally) *been denied.*" Included were their four point appeals guidelines. You are given 30 days from the DOS's desk date to appeal or start over.

**Forty Months Later** Long departed, the post delivered an unsolicited State Department "Official Business" flat postmarked August 10, **2015**. In it were inexplicably "discovered" documents regarding our Case No. F-2012-xxxxx, Segment: PRV-0001.

They indicated a DOS search, "*...conducted in another FOIA case has resulted in the retrieval of two documents responsive to your request.*" "*Where we have made excisions, the applicable exemptions are marked on each document.*" The cover letter was signed at the Director's level of the Office of Information Programs and Services and the pages were subjected to a Senior Review Authority named Lahiguera who only released them, "*in part*" for protection. Whose protection from what?

These documents, pertaining to our (still open) first quarter 2012 request, provided information that should have been originally released. The photocopying charges were oddly waived. Why this file had secretly stayed open was unclear, but everything written in 2012 was reversed. The following is what we received and this is the only book in which it is available.

**March 7, 2012**, Mr. Gillespie (TIGHAR) wrote Foreign Minister Tessie Lambourne in Kiribati: "*The announcement of the expedition will be made by the U.S. Secretary of State at a special event, in Washington on March 20. If we can get the Antiquities Management Agreement ready to sign by then we would be honored to have you and/or President Tong as our guest. We would cover all travel expense. The event on March 20 is sure to attract extensive media attention. Please say you'll come.*" And later, "*I am sure you'll agree, time is of the essence in getting the agreement reviewed and signed.*"[xc] Reviewed by whom? DOS?

This event had obviously been staged before anyone overseas was contacted. With just two weeks to go, the TIGHAR Group offered to pay for two round trip airfares whose second fare went to the Foreign Minister's spouse. So whose charitable contributions were in play?

**March 11,** it was announced the Kiribati President (2003-2016)

Anote Tong would not attend. The statement was cc: to five State Department employees providing historians with an idea of how important it was to get this right for Madame Secretary.

**March 13,** both the U.S. Deputy Director, Office for Australia, New Zealand and Pacific Island Affairs and the Deputy Assistant Secretary for East Asia & Pacific Affairs corresponded to finalize arrangements. One wonders what the General Accounting Office (GAO) says their hourly salary/benefit/pension time is worth.

The receipt of this documentation was clearly in response to this book's earlier editions indicating those airfares might be paid by the taxpayer. While we appreciate the opportunity to clarify 3.3 years later, it is also regrettable the DOS refused to provide documentation for the last week leading up to the event. So, we wondered who authorized this closed file release of information. I called the State Department in September, 2015.

When I got through, an experienced clerk indicated he had never seen anything like it. Documents sent on a file closed for 40 months was unprecedented without a new FOIA request. I asked for the information on the last week before the event, and that request was forwarded up to the divisional manager as was confirmed by e-mail. Not surprisingly they never got back. The need for all this covering conduct was that the 2016 presidential primary election was looming and unbeknownst to us this book wound up with that level of attention.

———

*"We see ourselves as sort of a Pacific manifestation of Monty Python and the Holy Grail."*

TIGHAR to Herbert Traube – *Deputy Director, U.S. State Department Office for Australia, New Zealand and the Pacific Islands – March 13, 2012.*

FBI Lab Analysis Report regarding materials submitted by The TIGHAR Group. The Bureau's post analysis directive:

*"Also advised* (the FBI)*...press office not to participate in person at any scheduled press conference arranged by TIGHAR."*

~ Department of Justice File 62-48646 ~

Amelia Earhart

# "Interpretive Ambiguity"

National Geographic Society's Gold
Medal awarded by President Herbert Hoover

(This book) *'Tis no sinister nor awkward claim*
*Picked from the wormholes of long-vanished days,*
*Nor from the dust of old oblivion raked.*

Shakespeare in *Henry V*

Evidential Details

It is obvious that when you are out to prove a scenario you are saddled with an agenda. In direct response Mr. Gillespie stated he has no agenda, he just goes where the evidence leads. But somehow, someway, it invariably leads to his personal Castaway's Theory. TIGHAR's need has always been to prove a scenario that never existed. And given the pressure of eleven failures, these efforts could become unprincipled.

Remember, TIGHAR has money to pay back, a reputation to prop up, and the potential to develop big income. So for the TIGHAR Group, if you furnish any animal sample to a laboratory and the scientists declare it is not from homo sapien – that rule out is science. TIGHAR science.

Reference is made to the turtle bone into a human finger bone lab analysis. Then there was the Touch DNA flim-flam. At the laboratory there were employees who were subject to salary, benefit and pension packages during the Great Recession of the early 21st Century.

To understand how this works, you <u>must believe</u>:
1. That repeat business potential does not talk;
2. An individual conflict of interest is impossible;
3. That fake news from a technician cannot happen;
4. That getting caught with a slightly altered lab result will not be explained away with an forcefully repeated apology;
5. In summation, you must believe that, "*some deceitful practice or willful devise, resorted to with intent to deprive another*"[xci] cannot happen in a TIGHAR selected laboratory where they pay the bill. Remember, driver Henri Paul's conflicting laboratory blood sample data in this book's Introduction:

**McMoneagle - You only have to switch the samples... Or, pay off the guy who is doing the tests. You could also conceivably rig the test equipment.**

After TIGHAR's 2010 trip, it was announced they needed $3 to $4 million for a deep-sea mission. But after Hillary Clinton's federal extravaganza, that number dropped to $2 million. Every time the TIGHAR Group said something it made news. Peculiar to the United States, the media is managed to drive the market in one direction. So when the Castaway failures occurred, a coordinated news blackout followed.

When an enhanced image was handed to TIGHAR by a "supporter" in 2013, the whole Internet lit up for TIGHAR's latest find! Speaking to MSN News, TIGHAR's Ric Gillespie said this new discovery was a surprise! Then he exuberantly declared:

*"This could be it! We know it's the right size, the right shape and in the right place to be the wreckage."* *"This is detective work. It's Sherlock Holmes stuff."* (Fiction)

So an *MSN News Rumors* headline put the question:

*"Does a grainy image show what's left of the pioneering pilot's aircraft, or is it just the latest publicity stunt to get in line for research cash?"*

Naturally this "grainy image" was also discredited but contributions did come in. And again, we are not able to print it under TIGHAR's lawsuit threat. Which brings us to why:

To support TIGHAR, you <u>must believe</u> that the current American Press Establishment would never be willing to mislead the public into spending millions of dollars! These are the issues.

• The country has witnessed coordinated press efforts and once they sing out about "smoking gun" Castaways evidence, the calculation is that considerable press power will manipulate an unsuspecting public to take it at face value. This belief was made abundantly clear with the History Channel's™ 2017 "lost evidence" documentary Earhart's "new" picture scam;

• Third party exploration efforts will be priced out when applying for TIGHAR's SOHO printer Nikumaroro license;

• The only certainty is that for the consumers who wasted their money on a Castaways "find" - there will be no refund;

• Against this backdrop, the public, and historians, will have to <u>demand</u> third party verification on any TIGHAR "find." But as set-up, verification cannot happen with a press monopoly. All the bases have been covered.

So, going into 2014, TIGHAR's web site announced their latest theory to be rested. No longer referring exclusively to west end waters, they declared something impossible given their previous PhD level TIGHAR Science Castaways parameters:

*As we discuss, plan, and conduct the Niku VIII (2015) expedition, we'll be referencing <u>various parts</u> of Nikumaroro and <u>the surrounding waters</u>* (enter the two ship strategy off different shores).

# To the Debris Field

The Amelia Earhart mystery is in need of what is known as "feedback." The Gallagher Curvature debris field needs to be marked with a six-foot orange buoy and here is how. Go where the Pentagon would have sent the Naval Air.

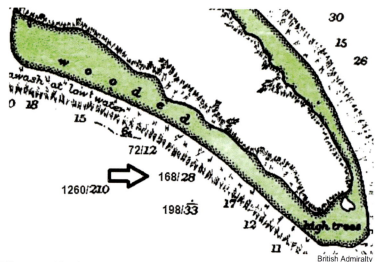

British Admiralty

Nikumaroro/Gardner Island's Gallagher Curvature. The numbers to the left are in feet, to the right in fathoms. The arrow represents Earhart's approach as, turning into the sun, she attempted to nestle the aircraft up along the shoreline. Our first verification of the **page 78** data (first line) came when we realized the water's depth was at 1260 feet behind the arrow, but only dropped from 168 to 198 feet in front of the arrow. Slightly further out is the debris field underwater ridge (p. 79).

The one-way air mileage - Honolulu to Kanton (airports HNL–CIS) is 1901 miles (3,059km). The distance, Kanton to Gardener Island is approximately 200 miles (322km). This means a plane can be in the waters off the southeast coast in about 90 minutes from Kanton.

Another route enabling a shorter range aircraft is Honolulu to the Palmyra Atoll Airfield (PLPA) with its unattended 5,000 foot (1524m) runway. This distance is 957 miles (1540k) which is about half way to Nikumaroro.

**First** – Review the numbers. The location is, **approximately 2,283 feet from the tip of** (the) **exposed reef**. That means 2,283 feet along the South Aukaraime - Gallagher Curvature - high tide coast line from the eastern point. The figures on the map reveal the plane will be found, **1300 to 1400 feet off the outside reef**, near the middle of the last segment of the island, at an approximate **650 foot depth**;

**Second** – Buy the original TIGHAR southeastern sea floor mapping graphic. Purchasing may reflect a quick pricing revision with a concentrated telephone cross examination;

**Caution**: This picture was available to view on TIGHAR's web site but, reacting to our scenario, the picture has been cut in half. You will need the whole image to see the east end underwater ridge.

**Third** – Put a seaplane down in the water with one of the various makes of magnetic detection rental equipment costing ~$1000/week (2017). With picture in hand, set-up to troll (east-west) along the upward sea floor curvature showing 650 feet of water. A more expensive stereoscopic underwater terrain analyzer would be preferable;

**Fourth** - Start trolling the area. The rows will depend on the swath width of the metal detector. The process can be likened to a field combine at harvest. Simply start trolling up and back. Remember, **it is all lying within a circle with a radius of about 75 yards.** A diameter of 150 yards generates a circle of just over 470 square yards ($393m^2$). Once you get a ping home in on it, as it could be a trail that leads to the debris field. Out of the whole South Pacific, the debris is in less than 3 length x 2 width football fields. It should be less than one day's trolling.

Once you find the debris field, mark it with GPS and anchor a large orange buoy securely prevent drift. Fly back to your prearranged fuel depot. The price for a Kiribati government official to accompany the venture in 2015 was US $15,000.00.

And finally, consider this book as analogous to a piece of open source software. It awaits precise GPS debris field coordinates to finalize this investigation and answer the mystery of Amelia Earhart's disappearance.


*Historians wage a constant battle in trying to pin down reality. How they are being treated by the political, social, or religious pressures in the now of their time and place will usually dictate how they will report reality. Since it is the political, social, and religious environment that pays for their work, endorses their findings, and passes judgment on them, who can blame for doing otherwise.*

~Joseph W. McMoneagle – The Ultimate Time Machine~

# Bibliography

- Bellarts, Leo G., Record Group 200 - National Archives, Washington, D.C.
- Brink, Randall - *Lost Star – The Search for Amelia Earhart*, W.W. Norton & Company, 1993
- Butler, Susan - *East to the Dawn – The Life of Amelia Earhart*; Addison Wesley Longman, 1997
- Carroll, Andrew - *Letters of a Nation – A Collection of Extraordinary American Letters*; Kodansha International Limited, 1997
- Chater, Eric H. - General Manager, Guinea Airways Limited. Correspondence with M.E. Griffin, Placer Management Limited, San Francisco, California dated Lae, New Guinea July 25, 1937
- The United Kingdom's Hydrographic Office website
- Faheys – Ships and Aircraft of the US Fleet - War Edition
- Goerner, Fred - *The Search for Amelia Earhart*, Doubleday & Company, 1966
- Lovell, Mary S. - *The Sound of Wings - The Life of Amelia Earhart*; St. Martin's Press, 1989
- McRae Ron, *Mind Wars – The True Story of Secret Government Research into the Military Potential of Psychic Weapons*; St. Martin's Press, 1984
- Morrissey, Murial Earhart - Oral History Collection - *The Reminiscences of Murial Earhart Morrissey,* Columbia University
- MSN on line News Services
- Pellegreno, Ann Holtgren, *World Flight – The Earhart Trail*; Iowa State University Press/Ames, 1971
- Purdue University Libraries, West Lafayette, Indiana - The Amelia Earhart Digital Collection in the Earhart Special Collections Library
- Putnam, George Palmer - *Soaring Wings - A Biography of Amelia Earhart*; Hartcourt, Brace and Company, Inc., 1939
- Smith, Len Young and Roberson, G. Gale - *Business Law, Uniform Commercial Code, Third Edition*; West Publishing Company, 1971
- The TIGHAR Group, Earhart Project Research Bulletin #71; The Riddle of Artifact #2-2-V-1; May 22, 2014
- Tighar Tracks - Volume 12 Number 2/3 October, 1996
- United States Central Intelligence Agency - www.cia.gov/cia/publications/factbook/geos/hq/html
- United States Naval Archives; Cablegrams between George Putnam and Secretary of Commerce Daniel Roper, 1937

# Part III

Author

The last air-worthy Lockheed Electra 10.

*...as a result of my own previous exposure to this* (remote viewing) *community I became persuaded that war can almost always be traced to a failure in intelligence, and that therefore the strongest weapon for peace is good intelligence.*

~ H. E. Puthoff, PhD. ~

Founder and First Director (1972-1985) the Military
Intelligence Black Ops program known as Operation Star Gate.

# JOSEPH W. MCMONEAGLE
### CW2, US Army, **Owner/Executive Director** of Intuitive Intelligence Applications, Inc.

Mr. McMoneagle has 34 years of professional expertise in research and development, in numerous multi-level technical systems, the paranormal, and the social sciences. Experience includes: experimental protocol design, collection and evaluation of statistical information, prototype design and testing, Automatic Data Processing equipment and technology interface, management, and data systems analysis for mainframe, mini-mainframe, and desktop computer systems supporting information collection and analysis for intelligence purposes.

He is currently owner and Executive Director of Intuitive Intelligenc Applications, Inc., which has provided support to multiple research facilities and corporations with a full range of collection applications using Anamolous Cognition (AC) in the production of original and cutting edge information. He is a full time Research Associate with The Laboratories for Fundamental Research, Cognitive Sciences Laboratory, Palo Alto, California, where he has provided consulting support to research and development in remote viewing for 16+ years. As a consultant to SRI-International and Science Applications International Corporation, Inc. from 1984 through 1995, he participated in protocol design, statistical information collection, R&D evaluations, as well as thousands of remote viewing trials in support of both experimental research as well as active intelligence operations for what is now known as Project (Operation) STARGATE. He is well versed with developmental theory, methods of application, and current training technologies for remote viewing, as currently applied under strict laboratory controls and oversight.

During his career, Mr. McMoneagle has provided professsional intelligence and creative/innovative informational support to the Central Intelligence Agency, Defense Intelligence Agency, National Security Agency, Drug Enforcement Agency, Secret Service, Federal Bureau of Investigation, United States Customs, the National Security Council, most major commands within the Department of Defense, and hundreds of other individuals, companies, and corporations. He is the only one who has successfully demonstrated his ability more than two dozen times, by doing a live remote viewing, double-blind and under controls while on-camera for national networks/labs in four countries.

Mr. McMoneagle has also been responsible for his Military Occupational Specialty at Army Headquarters level, to include control and management of both manned and unmanned sites within the Continental United States, and overseas. He was re-sponsible for all tactical and strategic equipment tasking, including aircraft and vehicles, development of new and current technology, planning, support and maintenance, funding, training, and person-nel. He has performed responsibly in international and intra-service negotiations and agreements in support of six national level intelligence agencies, and has acted as a direct consultant to the Commanding General, United States Army Intelligence and Security Command (INSCOM), Washington D.C., as well as the Army Chief of Staff for Intelligence (ACSI), Pentagon. Other employment has included, Assistant to the Security Officer for a multi-billion dollar overseas intelligence facility, with responsibilities that included physical plant communications, personnel, and technology security; as well as counter-terrorist and counter-intelligence operations. He has served as the Detachment Com-mander at two remote intelligence collection sites overseas, providing field intelligence collection, analysis and reporting at theater, region, country, and city levels. He has also served on an Air and Sea Rescue team, in Long Range Reconnaissance, as a Quick Reaction Strike Force team leader, and rifleman. He has earned 28 military decorations and numerous awards…

| | |
|---|---|
| KHAQQ DE NRUI ANS 3105 KCS WID A3 HW OUR SIG QSA? CA / UNANSWD | 34-41 |
| LSNIN 3105 / NIL - CRM TUNIN UP T16 FER XMISION TO NMC | XX 42 |
| NMC V NRUI P AR, 12600 / UNANSWD | XX-43 |
| KHAQQ TO ITASCA WE ARE ON THE LINE 157 337 XX WL REPT MSG WE WL REPT | N ES S |
| THIS ON 6210 KCS WAIT, 3105/A3 S5 (?/KHAQQ XMISION WE ARE RUNNING | ONXXS LINE |
| LSNIN 6210 KCS / KHAQQ DE NRUI HRD U OK ON 3105 KCS XX, 7500 | 44-6 |

Amelia Earhart's final communication shown as aircraft radio KHAQQ.

# Human Use

This is a quick but fascinating overview on the formally classified application controversy surrounding the Army's Human Use Policies developed to protect soldiers from classified experimentation.

----------

"In February 1979, the General Counsel, the Army's top lawyer, declared [the RV Program code named] Grill Flame activities constitute Human Use." The Unit, "… was in the middle of the [Congressional authorization] process in March 1979 when the Human Use determination was reversed by the Army Surgeon General's Human Use Subjects Research Review Board. Their decision …trumped the Army General Counsel's ruling…"

"On November 20, the Surgeon General's board changed its mind and decided that Grill Flame did indeed involve Human Use. It took until February 1, 1982 to get final approval from the (Joint Chiefs of Staff) Secretary of the Army to continue operations."[18]

New candidates were then issued a warning by a Major General before being accepted into the 902nd black-ops Intelligence Unit.

"Among other things, they noted that if the candidate joined the project, he would be exposed to psychic phenomena at a level and with a frequency that most people had never experienced before. As a result, he might change in certain ways. Ultimately, no harm should come to him, but he might have a new perspective on himself, his marriage, the universe. In a sense, he might become a new man, and a new husband."

The candidate and his wife were advised to talk, "…this over before they made the final commitment to go to Fort Meade."[19]

[18] Smith, Paul H., *Reading the Enemy's Mind – Inside Star Gate, America's Psychic Espionage Program*; Tor Non-fiction, 2005; p. 118

[19] Schnabel, Jim, *Remote Viewers: The Secret History of America's Psychic Spies*; Dell Non-Fiction, 1997, p. 270

# A Chinese Encounter

The United States is not the only nation to study and use Remote Viewing. Below is a story allowing enthusiasts and skeptics alike a rare look at an event inside the Unit during the middle 1980s.

-----------

"The first time it happened was right after [Major] General Stubblebine had briefed me on the project and said that I would be contacted. The next week I was working mid-shift, and one of the afternoons, I lay down for a nap. In that nap, I had a really shallow and lame dream about something I can't remember now. But at one point, right over the top of that dream there was what appeared to be a semi-translucent visual of three people.

One was a very respectable, businesslike slender man in a suit. A second was a very burly, stocky man, also in a suit, and with a very "Texas farmer" face. The third was an...Oriental girl... (I find it impossible to tell the age of oriental women). She was following along behind the two men and watching.

The men came up to me and talked about something, but I couldn't hear them. The girl was standing behind the two men, listening. The faces were very clear. Clear enough that when the two men actually came to [the INSCOM Base[20] in] Augsburg [Germany] to interview me, I recognized them immediately. I could have picked them out of a crowd on the sidewalk. I didn't think anything of the fact that the girl wasn't with them. It would have been odd to have her on a military trip overseas. I thought she was probably someone in the unit.

Months later, when I got to the unit, she wasn't there. I asked about her and neither the director nor Joe [McMoneagle] (the two men who came to interview me) knew who I was talking about. I figured that it was just an AOL (STRAY CAT)[21] and blew it off.

About a year later, I was doing a practice target. The target was a museum at Arizona State University (I didn't know

---

[20] INSCOM is the abbreviation for the Army's Intelligence and Security Command.

[21] A Stray Cat is a viewer acronym describing the Subconscious Transfer of Recollections, Anxieties, and Yearnings to Consciously Accessible Thought.

that - I only had [coordinate] numbers). I was describing things lying in glass topped cases, with the cases up on legs and stands, all arranged around the room for easy access, when I noticed that someone at the target site was looking straight at me, as though she could see me. It startled me, and for probably the only time ever, I wasn't startled OUT of the session, but deeper into it.

I looked back at her, and realized that it was the same girl who had been following the director and Joe in my earlier "dream", back in Augsburg. I looked directly at her, and started to say hello, but then she realized that I could see her, too, and she half turned, and disappeared. That threw me out of the session.

Fortunately, [Captain] Paul Smith was my monitor, and ever the curious one, when I told him what had happened, he said, "*Let's follow her and see where she went.*" Through a series of very impromptu movement commands, we finally located her back at the place where she worked ... the Chinese psychic intelligence effort.

She appeared in some of my sessions after that, but rarely. I tried to find her several times, and a few of them succeeded. Apparently, what they defined as "session" and what we defined as "session" weren't the same. Anyway, over time, we struck up somewhat of a standoffish acquaintance.

About a year after that, I hadn't bumped into her again, so I did a session specifically to find her. She was then in college in a very large city, and evidently out of the government's protect altogether. When I found her, she acknowledged my presence, and very strongly desired that we not have further contact. I backed out of the session, and haven't tried again, since. Don't cha love war stories?"

Oct. 1, 1998 e-mail from Leonard Buchanan – Former Operation Star Gate Database Manager, 902 Military Intelligence Unit at Fort Meade, Maryland Owner of Problems>Solutions>Innovations, Inc.

--------------

For more information, see, *China's Super Psychics* by Paul Dong and Thomas Raffill; Marlowe & Co. New York, 1997

Amelia Earhart

# Remote Viewing Protocols

Surrounding the military's RV Session Protocols are the Operational Flow Protocols. The tasking agency was the "Customer" whose identity was strictly withheld to avoid inferences leading to Analytic Overlay. First published here, this process was highly classified for over two decades.

---------

"In actual fact, there was pretty much a different work set-up every time we changed directors in the military unit which was pretty often as projects go. As a result, the "ideal plan" was never adhered to. Many times, we had to sort of switch horse in midstream. Anyway, here is the "ideal" workflow:

The **CUSTOMER** (Targeting Agency) comes to the unit director with a tasking.

The **UNIT DIRECTOR** meets with the customer and:

1) makes absolutely certain that the customer knows what CRV is and isn't – what it will and won't do.

2) looks the customer's problem over to see that it is the type of work we are best suited for. If not, he suggests a different solution for them.

If so, he then:

3) gets rid of the customer's "test" questions which only take up time and effort and accomplish nothing.

4) gets rid of the unnecessary questions – just fluff questions which the customer would like to have answered.

5) makes certain the questions asked are questions the customer really wants the answers to. There are LOTS of times when the customer will ask, "Who killed the victim", when the information he really wants is, "Where can we find the evidence that will show who killed the victim?"

6) agrees in writing on a set of basic questions which will be answered, once all the fluff and confusion is gotten out of the way.

7) makes certain that the Customer knows that these questions will be answered, and that other information will be provided, if it is found. However, if it isn't found, then the viewers are only responsible for what is being tasked. Follow-on questions will have to be asked later.

# Evidential Details

8) explains to the Customer the need for accurate feedback.

9) gets a definite commitment from the Customer that such feedback will be given, on each and every viewer's answer(s) to each and every question.

10) sets a commitment date for providing the answers. This must be a realistic date. Every Customer wants answers right now or yesterday, but the unit director needs to impress on the Customer that there are other customers who also have time limits of now or yesterday, and that reality must figure into the planning, like it or not.

11) provides the final list of questions to the Project Officer, along with any background information about the case gained from the customer.

The **PROJECT OFFICER** studies the background information and tasked questions and:

1) determines the main subject matter for each question.

2) decides the project number and fills out all the preliminary paperwork required for starting a new project.

3) provides the list of subjects to the Data Base Manager. The Data Base Manager looks up each information category in the data base and provides the Project Manager with a separate list of Viewers' names as suggested Viewers for each question.

4) determines which Viewers and Monitors should work on each question.

5) looks at the Viewers' and Monitors' existing schedules and determines the project's time line. He may even do a Pert chart to make scheduling easier.

6) "translates" each question into neutral wording.

7) notifies each Monitor and Viewer of the work schedule change.

8) generates an official tasking sheet to hand to each Monitor.

The **MONITOR** receives the tasking and coordinates from the Project Officer, along with any background information the Project Officer thinks the Monitor should know to help the Viewer better perform a productive session. The Monitor then:

1) makes certain he knows the Viewer's likes and dislikes, quirks, micro-movements, etc. If not, these are either looked up or found out from another Monitor who is more familiar with the Viewer.

2) gets information from the Database Manager about the Viewer's strengths and weaknesses. While this carries the danger of a "self-fulfilling prophecy", the Monitor is hopefully trained enough to use

134

the information for formatting the session, rather than for guiding and leading the Viewer. If the Monitor is not this well trained, this step is passed up.

3) prepares the session workplace.

4) goes through the session with the Viewer.

5) helps the Viewer write the summary, if necessary.

6) after the paperwork is all done, provides both the Viewer's transcript and his (the Monitor's) session notes to the Analyst.

The **ANALYST** receives the paperwork and:

1) familiarizes himself with all the background knowledge.

2) collects the papers from all Viewer/Monitor pairs.

3) looks into his own notes on each and every Viewer to see work profiles (prone to using imagery, prone to using allegories, etc.). The Database Manager can be of help in this step.

4) performs analysis on the session (see the Analyst's Manual).

5) writes up his reports, critiques, summaries, etc. and provides it to the Report Writer.

The **REPORT WRITER** receives all the information from the Analyst and:

1) familiarizes himself with all the available background information.

2) familiarizes himself with all the Analyst's finding, interpretations and comments.

3) writes the final report (see the Report Writer's Manual)

NOTE!!! This includes taking the finalized answer to each Viewer to make certain that what is being reported is what the Viewer actually meant to say.

4) provides the final report to the Project Officer.

The **PROJECT OFFICER** then:

1) receives the finalized answers to each question after the session has been performed, analyzed and prepared for reporting.

2) gives final approval on the final report.

3) passes the final report to the Unit Director for delivery to the Customer.

The **UNIT DIRECTOR** then:

1) contacts the Customer and sets a date and time to go over the report. Information is not given ad hoc over the phone, nor is an "executive summary" provided.

2) meets with the Customer to provide the report.

3) once again makes certain that the Customer understands the

CRV process, strengths and limitations.

4) explains what happened, and how each answer was obtained.

5) points out to the Customer that each question has a "dependability rating" beside it which will tell the Customer what each Viewer's track record is on each specific answer to each type of question. He explains how this "dependability rating" can be used by the Customer as an aid to making decisions from the information provided.

6) sets – in writing – a hard and definite "drop dead" date for feedback.

7) if/when feedback comes in, provides it to the Project Officer who handled the case.

8) if feedback doesn't come in, or is received incorrectly, it is returned to the Customer to either, "dun him" for feedback, or to re-explain how feed-back needs to be provided, formatted, etc.

The **PROJECT OFFICER** then:

1) evaluates each Viewer's response to each question against the feedback.

2) provides an evaluation to each Viewer.

3) provides accurate data to the Database Manager for input into the database.

4) completes all summary paperwork for the project.

5) organizes all related paperwork, checks it for completeness, and prepares it for final storage and filing.

The **DATABASE MANAGER**:

1) inputs all received information into the database.

2) "massages" the database to provide information to those who need it. This includes the Training Officer and all Trainers.

3) maintains quality control on the data going in. "Garbage in – garbage out".

The **TRAINING OFFICER**:

1) schedules training times and facilities.

2) keeps evaluation reports on the Trainers.

The **TRAINER**:

1) accompanies new Viewers through the training process, analyzing their needs and    progress every step of the way (see Trainers Manual).

2) makes and keeps records of the Viewer Student's "natural micro-movements". These will be provided to the Monitors along with a Viewer Student's profile of strengths and weakness.

3) advises management of the Viewer Student's progress and advises as to the student's best possible "training track" for providing the most useful and productive Viewer possible.

Needless to say, this is an overview, and not a complete list of responsibilities and obligations. For example, it doesn't cover what goes on in follow-on tasking, etc.

July 23, 1998 e-mail from: Leonard Buchanan– Former Operational Database Manager at the 902nd Military Intelligence Unit - Fort Meade, Maryland and Owner of Problems> Solutions>Innovations, Inc.

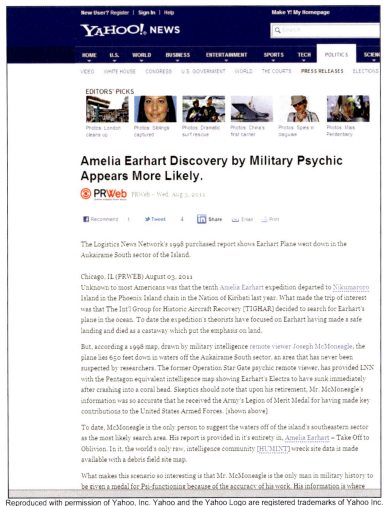

# Beginnings

This details the basis for the original black ops program funding. For readers interested in the data that justified continued Congressional spending, this overview of U.S. Military History is recommended.

## CIA-Initiated Remote Viewing at Stanford Research Institute

by H. E. Puthoff, Ph.D.[22]
Institute for Advanced Studies at Austin
4030 Braker Lane W., #300
Austin, Texas 78759-5329

Abstract - In July 1995 the CIA declassified, and approved for release, documents revealing its sponsorship in the 1970s of a program at Stanford Research Institute in Menlo Park, CA, to determine whether such phenomena as remote viewing "might have any utility for intelligence collection" [1]. Thus began disclosure to the public of a two-decade-plus involvement of the intelligence community in the investigation of so-called para-psychological or psi phenomena. Presented here by the program's Founder and first Director (1972 - 1985) is the early history of the program, including discussion of some of the first, now declassified, results that drove early interest.

---

[22] Harold Puthoff received his BS and MS Degrees in Electrical Engineering at the University of Florida and a PhD from Stanford University in 1967. He went on to work at the National Security Agency at Fort Meade, Maryland as an Army engineer studying, lasers, high-speed computers, and fiber optics. He is the inventor of the tunable infra-red laser. He spent three years as a naval officer and worked eight years in the Microwave Laboratory at Stanford. Puthoff has over 31 technical papers published on such topics as electron-beam devices, lasers and quantum zero-point-energy effects. He reportedly has patents issued in the areas of energy fields, laser, and communications. [author]

# Introduction

On April 17, 1995, President Clinton issued Executive Order Nr. 1995-4-17, entitled Classified National Security Information. Although in one sense the order simply reaffirmed much of what has been long-standing policy, in another sense there was a clear shift toward more openness. In the opening paragraph, for example, we read: "In recent years, however, dramatic changes have altered, although not eliminated, the national security threats that we confront. These changes provide a greater opportunity to emphasize our commitment to open Government." In the Classification Standards section of the Order this commitment is operationalized by phrases such as "If there is significant doubt about the need to classify information, it shall not be classified." Later in the document, in reference to information that requires continued protection, there even appears the remarkable phrase "In some exceptional cases, however, the need to protect such information may be outweighed by the public interest in disclosure of the information, and in these cases the information should be declassified."

A major fallout of this reframing of attitude toward classification is that there is enormous pressure on those charged with maintaining security to work hard at being responsive to reasonable requests for disclosure. One of the results is that FOIA (Freedom of Information Act) requests that have languished for months to years are suddenly being acted upon.[1]

One outcome of this change in policy is the government's recent admission of its two-decade-plus involvement in funding highly-classified, special access programs in remote viewing (RV) and related psi phenomena, first at Stanford Research Institute (SRI) and then at Science Applications International Corporation (SAIC), both in Menlo Park, CA, supplemented by various in-house government programs. Although almost all of the documentation remains yet classified, in July 1995 270 pages of SRI reports were declassified and released by the CIA, the program's first sponsor [2]. Thus, although through the years columns by Jack Anderson and others had claimed leaks of "psychic spy" programs with such exotic names as Grill Flame, Center Lane, Sunstreak and Star Gate, CIA's release of the SRI reports constitutes the first documented public admission of significant intelligence community involvement in the psi area.

As a consequence of the above, although I had founded the program in early 1972, and had acted as its Director until I left in 1985 to head up the Institute for Advanced Studies at Austin (at which point my colleague Ed May assumed responsibility as Director), it was not until 1995 that I found myself for the first time able to utter in a single sentence the connected acronyms CIA/SRI/RV. In this report I discuss the genesis of the program, report on some of the early, now declassified, results that drove early interest, and outline the general direction the program took as it expanded into a multi-year, multi-site, multi-million-dollar effort to determine whether such phenomena as remote viewing "might have any utility for intelligence collection" [1].

# Beginnings

In early 1972, I was involved in laser research at Stanford Research Institute (now called SRI International) in Menlo Park, CA. At that time I was also circulating a proposal to obtain a small grant for some research in quantum biology. In that proposal I had raised the issue whether physical theory as we knew it was capable of describing life processes, and had suggested some measurements involving plants and lower organisms [3]. This proposal was widely circulated, and a copy was sent to Cleve Backster in New York City who was involved in measuring the electrical activity of plants with standard polygraph equipment. New York artist Ingo Swann chanced to see my proposal during a visit to Backster's lab, and wrote me suggesting that if I were interested in investigating the boundary between the physics of the animate and inanimate, I should consider experiments of the parapsychological type. Swann then went on to describe some apparently successful experiments in psychokinesis in which he had participated at Prof. Gertrude Schmeidler's laboratory at the City College of New York. As a result of this correspondence I invited him to visit SRI for a week in June 1972 to demonstrate such effects, frankly, as much out of personal scientific curiosity as anything else.

Prior to Swann's visit I arranged for access to a well-shielded magneto-meter used in a quark-detection experiment in the Physics Department at Stanford University. During our visit to this laboratory, sprung as a surprise to Swann, he appeared to perturb the operation of the magnetometer, located in a vault below the floor of the building and shielded by mu-metal shielding, an aluminum container, copper shielding and a superconducting shield. As if to add insult to injury, he then went on to "remote view" the interior of the apparatus, rendering by drawing a reasonable facsimile of its rather complex (and heretofore unpublished) construction. It was this latter feat that impressed me perhaps even more than the former, as it also eventually did representatives of the intelligence community. I wrote up these observations and circulated it among my scientific colleagues in draft form of what was eventually published as part of a conference proceeding [4].

In a few short weeks a pair of visitors showed up at SRI with the above report in hand. Their credentials showed them to be from the CIA. They knew of my previous background as a Naval Intelligence Officer and then civilian employee at the National Security Agency (NSA) several years earlier, and felt they could discuss their concerns with me openly. There was, they told me, increasing concern in the intelligence community about the level of effort in Soviet parapsychology being funded by the Soviet security services [5]; by Western scientific standards the field was considered nonsense by most working scientists. As a result they had been on the lookout for a research laboratory outside of academia that could handle a quiet, low-profile classified investigation, and SRI appeared to fit the bill. They asked if I could arrange an opportunity for them to carry out some simple experiments with Swann, and, if the tests proved satisfactory, would I consider a pilot program along these lines? I agreed to consider this, and arranged for the requested tests. [2]

The tests were simple, the visitors simply hiding objects in a box and asking Swann to attempt to describe the contents. The results generated in these experiments are perhaps captured most eloquently by the following example. In one test Swann said "I see something small, brown and irregular, sort of like a leaf or some-thing that resembles it, except that it seems very much alive, like it's even moving!" The target chosen by one of the visitors turned out to be a small live moth, which indeed did look like a leaf. Although not all responses were quite so precise, nonetheless the integrated results were sufficiently impressive that in short order an eight-month, $49,909 Biofield Measurements Program was negotiated as a pilot study, a laser colleague Russell Targ who had had a long-time interest and involvement in parapsychology joined the program, and the experimental effort was begun in earnest.

## Early Remote Viewing Results

During the eight-month pilot study of remote viewing the effort gradually evolved from the remote viewing of symbols and objects in envelopes and boxes, to the remote viewing of local target sites in the San Francisco Bay area, demarked by outbound experimenters sent to the site under strict protocols devised to prevent artifactual results. Later judging of the results were similarly handled by double-blind protocols designed to foil artifactual matching. Since these results have been presented in detail elsewhere, both in the scientific literature [6-8] and in popular book format [9], I direct the interested reader to these sources. To summarize, over the years the back-and-forth criticism of protocols, refinement of methods, and successful replication of this type of remote viewing in independent laboratories [10-14], has yielded considerable scientific evidence for the reality of the phenomenon. Adding to the strength of these results was the discovery that a growing number of individuals could be found to demonstrate high-quality remote viewing, often to their own surprise, such as the talented Hella Hammid. As a separate issue, however, most convincing to our early program monitors were the results now to be described, generated under their own control.

First, during the collection of data for a formal remote viewing series targeting indoor laboratory apparatus and outdoor locations (a series eventually published in toto in the Proc. IEEE [7]), the CIA contract monitors, ever watchful for possible chicanery, participated as remote viewers themselves in order to critique the protocols. In this role three separate viewers, designated visitors V1 - V3 in the IEEE paper, contributed seven of the 55 viewings, several of striking quality. Reference to the IEEE paper for a comparison of descriptions/ drawings to pictures of the associated targets, generated by the contract monitors in their own viewings, leaves little doubt as to why the contract monitors came to the conclusion that there was something to remote viewing (see, for example, Figure 1 herein).

As summarized in the Executive Summary of the now-released Final Report [2] of the second year of the program, "The development of this capability at SRI has evolved to the point where visiting CIA personnel with no previous exposure to such concepts have performed well under controlled laboratory conditions (that is, generated target descriptions of sufficiently high quality to permit blind matching of descriptions to targets by independent judges)." What happened next, however, made even these results pale in comparison.

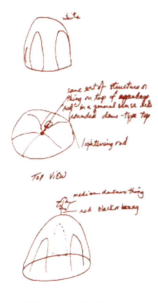

Figure 1 – Sketch
of target by VI

Figure 2 – Target
(merry-go-round)

# Coordinate Remote Viewing

To determine whether it was necessary to have a "beacon" individual at the target site, Swann suggested carrying out an experiment to remote view the planet Jupiter before the upcoming NASA Pioneer 10 fly by. In that case, much to his chagrin (and ours) he found a ring around Jupiter, and wondered if perhaps he had remote viewed Saturn by mistake. Our colleagues in astronomy were quite unimpressed as well, until the flyby revealed that an unanticipated ring did in fact exist. [3] Expanding the protocols yet further, Swann proposed a series of experiments in which the target was designated not by sending a "beacon" person to the target site, but rather by the use of geographical coordinates, latitude and longitude in degrees, minutes and seconds. Needless to say, this proposal seemed even more out-rageous than "ordinary" remote viewing. The difficulties in taking this proposal seriously, designing protocols to eliminate the possibility of a combination of globe memorization and eidetic or photographic memory, and so forth, are discussed in considerable detail in Reference [9]. Suffice it to say that investigation of this approach, which we designated Scanate (scanning by coordinate), eventually provided us with sufficient evidence to bring it up to the contract monitors and suggest a test under their control. A description of that test and its results, carried out in mid-1973 during the initial pilot study, are best presented by quoting directly from the Executive Summary of the Final Report of the second year's follow-up program [2]. The remote viewers were Ingo Swann and Pat Price, and the entire transcripts are available in the released documents [2].

In order to subject the remote viewing phenomena to a rigorous long distance test under external control, a request for geographical coordinates of a site unknown to subject and experimenters was forwarded to the OSI group responsible for threat analysis in this area. In response, SRI personnel received a set of geographical coordinates (latitude and longitude in degrees, minutes, and seconds) of a facility, hereafter referred to as the West Virginia Site. The experimenters then carried out a remote viewing experiment on a double-blind basis, that is, blind to experimenters as well as subject. The experiment had as its goal the determination of the utility of remote viewing under conditions approximating an operational scenario. Two subjects targeted on the site, a sensitive installation. One subject drew a detailed map of the building and grounds layout, the other provided information about the interior including code words, data subsequently verified by sponsor sources (report available from COTR).[4]

Since details concerning the site's mission in general, [5] and evaluation of the remote viewing test in particular, remain highly classified to this day, all that can be said is that interest in the client community was heightened considerably following this exercise.

Because Price found the above exercise so interesting, as a personal challenge he went on to scan the other side of the globe for a Communist Bloc equivalent and found one located in the Urals, the detailed description of which is also included in Ref. [2]. As with the West Virginia Site, the report for the Urals Site was also verified by personnel in the sponsor organization as being substantially correct.

What makes the West Virginia/Urals Sites viewings so remarkable is that these are not best-ever examples culled out of a longer list; these are literally the first two site-viewings carried out in a simulated operational-type scenario. In fact, for Price these were the very first two remote viewings in our program altogether, and he was invited to participate in yet further experimentation.

# Operational Remote Viewing (Semipalatinsk, USSR)

Midway through the second year of the program (July 1974) our CIA sponsor decided to challenge us to provide data on a Soviet site of ongoing operational significance. Pat Price was the remote viewer. A description of the remote viewing, taken from our declassified final report [2], reads as given below. I cite this level of detail to indicate the thought that goes into such an "experiment" to minimize cueing while at the same time being responsive to the requirements of an operational situation. Again, this is not a "best-ever" example from a series of such viewings, but rather the very first operational Soviet target concerning which we were officially tasked. "To determine the utility of remote viewing under operational conditions, a long-distance remote viewing experiment was carried out on a sponsor designated target of current interest, an unidentified research center at Semipalatinsk, USSR.

This experiment, carried out in three phases, was under direct control of the COTR. To begin the experiment, the COTR furnished map coordinates in degrees, minutes and seconds. The only additional information provided was the designation of the target as an R&D test facility. The experimenters then closeted themselves with Subject S1, gave him the map coordinates and indicated the designation of the target as an R&D test facility. A remote-viewing experiment was then carried out. This activity constituted Phase I of the experiment.

Figure 3 shows the subject's graphic effort for building layout; Figure 4 shows the subject's particular attention to a multistory gantry crane he observed at the site. Both results were obtained by the experimenters on a double-blind basis before exposure to any additional COTR-held information, thus eliminating the possibility of cueing. These results were turned over to the client representatives for evaluation. For comparison, an artist's rendering of the site as known to the COTR (but not to the experimenters until later) is shown in Figure 5.

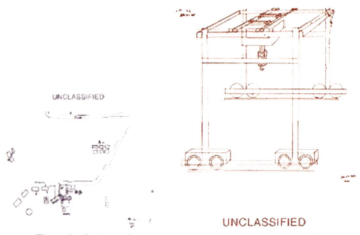

Figure 3 - Subject effort
at building layout

Figure 4 - Subject effort
construction crane

Were the results not promising, the experiment would have stopped at this point. Description of the multistory crane, however, a relatively unusual target item, was taken as indicative of possible target acquisition. Therefore, Phase II was begun, defined by the subject being made "witting" (of the client) by client representatives who introduced themselves to the subject at that point; Phase II also included a second round of experimentation on the Semipalatinsk site with direct participation of client representatives in which further data were obtained and evaluated. As preparation for this phase, client representatives purposely kept themselves blind to all but general knowledge of the target site to minimize the possibility of cueing. The Phase II effort was focused on the generation of physical data that could be independently verified by other client sources, thus providing a calibration of the process.

The end of Phase II gradually evolved into the first part of Phase III, the generation of unverifiable data concerning the Semipalatinsk site not available to the client, but of operational interest nonetheless. Several hours of tape transcript and a notebook of drawings were generated over a two-week period.

The data describing the Semipalatinsk site were evaluated by the sponsor, and are contained in a separate report. In general, several details concerning the salient technology of the Semipalatinsk site appeared to dovetail with data from other sources, and a number of specific large structural elements were correctly described. The results contained noise along with the signal, but were nonetheless clearly differentiated from the chance results that were generated by control subjects in comparison experiments carried out by the COTR."

For discussion of the ambiance and personal factors involved in carrying out this experiment, along with further detail generated as Price (see Figure 6) "roamed" the facility, including detailed comparison of Price's RV-generated information with later determined "ground-truth reality," see the accompanying article by Russell Targ in the Journal of Scientific Exploration <http:// www. jse.com/>, Vol. 10, No. 1.

Additional experiments having implications for intelligence concerns were carried out, such as the remote viewing of cipher machine type apparatus, and the RV-sorting of sealed envelopes to differentiate those that contained letters with secret writing from those that did not. To discuss these here in detail would take us too far afield, but the interested reader can follow up by referring to the now-declassified project documents [2].

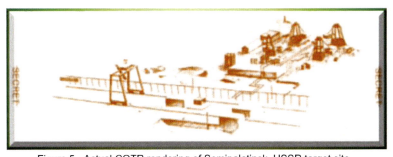

Figure 5 - Actual COTR rendering of Semipalatinsk, USSR target site.

## Follow-on Programs

The above discussion brings us up to the end of 1975. As a result of the material being generated by both SRI and CIA remote viewers, interest in the program in government circles, especially within the intelligence community, intensified consider-ably and led to an ever increasing briefing schedule. This in turn led to an ever-increasing number of clients, contracts and tasking, and therefore expansion of the program to a multi-client base, and eventually to an integrated joint-services program under single-agency (DIA)[6] leadership. To meet the demand for the increased level of effort we first increased our professional staff by inviting Ed May to join the program in 1976, then screened and added to the program a cadre of remote viewers as consultants, and let subcontracts to increase our scope of activity.

As the program expanded, in only a very few cases could the client's identities and program tasking be revealed. Examples include a NASA-funded study negotiated early in the program by Russ Targ to determine whether the internal state of an electronic random-number-generator could be detected by RV processes [16], and a study funded by the Naval Electronics Systems Com-mand to determine whether attempted remote viewing of distant light flashes would induce correlated changes in the viewer's brainwave (EEG) production [17]. For essentially all other projects, during my 14-yr. tenure at SRI, however, the identity of the clients and most of the tasking were classified and remain so today. (The exception was the occasional privately funded study.) We are told, however, that further declassification and release of much of this material is almost certain to occur.

What can be said, then, about further development of the program in the two decades following 1975?[7] In broad terms it can be said that much of the SRI effort was directed not so much toward developing an operational U.S. capability, but rather toward assessing the threat potential of its use against the U.S. by others.

The words 'threat assessment' were often used to des-cribe the program's purpose during its development, especially during the early years. As a result, much of the remote-viewing activity was carried out under conditions where ground-truth reality was a priori known or could be determined, such as the description of U.S. facilities and technological developments, the timing of rocket test firings and underground nuclear tests, and the location of individuals and mobile units. And, of course, we were responsive to requests to provide assistance during such events as the loss of an airplane or the taking of hostages, relying on the talents of an increasing cadre of remote-viewer/ consultants, some well-known in the field such as Keith Harary, and many who have not surfaced publicly until recently, such as Joe McMoneagle

Figure 6 - Left to right: Christopher Green, [23] Pat Price,[24] and Hal Puthoff. Picture taken following a successful experiment involving glider-ground RV.

One might ask whether in this program RV-generated information was ever of sufficient significance as to influence decisions at a policy level. This is of course impossible to determine unless policymakers were to come forward with a statement in the affirmative. One example of a possible candidate is a study we performed at SRI during the Carter administration debates concerning proposed deployment of the mobile MX missile system. In that scenario missiles were to be randomly

---

[23] Dr. Christopher Green MD. Neurophysiology, received the CIA's National Intelligence Medal as a Scientific Advisory Board Member to the CIA's Directorate of Intelligence.

[24] One of the finest remote viewers ever, Pat Price, a former police commissioner and councilman in Burbank, CA, came to the Government's attention when he viewed officers, interiors, and files at the virtually unknown, nuclear hardened Naval Satellite Intelligence site in West Virginia. When the Pentagon was shown the data, Price was interrogated by the U.S. Defense Investigative Service who demanded to know who had breached security and how they did it. He is reputed to be the only viewer that could read numbers and letters on a target. Later he viewed inside the Soviet installation at Mount Narodnaya in the Ural Mountains. He went on to work for the CIA and is reputed to have died of a heart attack in July of 1975, in Las Vegas. Even though he was supposedly dead on arrival at the hospital, no autopsy was performed. Suspicions have always existed about the truth of his death. [author]

shuffled from silo to silo in a silo field, in a form of high-tech shell game. In a computer simulation of a twenty-silo field with randomly -assigned (hidden) missile locations, we were able, using RV-generated data, to show rather forcefully that the application of a sophisticated statistical averaging technique (sequential sampling) could in principle permit an adversary to defeat the system. I briefed these results to the appropriate offices at their request, and a written report with the technical details was widely circulated among groups responsible for threat analysis [18], and with some impact. What role, if any, our small contribution played in the mix of factors behind the enormously complex decision to cancel the program will probably never be known, and must of course a priori be considered in all likelihood negligible. Nonetheless, this is a prototypical example of the kind of tasking that by its nature potentially had policy implications.

Even though the details of the broad range of experiments, some brilliant successes, many total failures, have not yet been released, we have nonetheless been able to publish summaries of what was learned in these studies about the overall characteristics of remote viewing, as in Table 5 of Reference [8]. Furthermore, over the years we were able to address certain questions of scientific interest in a rigorous way and to publish the results in the open literature. Examples include the apparent lack of attenuation of remote viewing due to seawater shielding (submersible experiments) [8], the amplification of RV performance by use of error-correcting coding techniques [19, 20], and the utility of a technique we call associational remote viewing (ARV) to generate useful predictive information [21].8

As a sociological aside, we note that the overall efficacy of remote viewing in a program like this was not just a scientific issue. For example, when the Semipalatinsk data described earlier was forwarded for analysis, one group declined to get involved because the whole concept was unscientific nonsense, while a second group declined because, even though it might be real, it was possibly demonic; a third group had to be found. And, as in the case of public debate about such phenomena, the program's image was on occasion as likely to be damaged by an over enthusiastic supporter, as by a detractor. Personalities, politics and personal biases were always factors to be dealt with.

## Official Statements/Perspectives

With regard to admission by the government of its use of remote viewers under operational conditions, officials have on occasion been relatively forthcoming. President Carter, in a speech to college students in Atlanta in September 1995, is quoted by Reuters as saying that during his administration a plane went down in Zaire, and a meticulous sweep of the African terrain by American spy satellites failed to locate any sign of the wreckage. It was then "without my knowledge" that the head of the CIA (Adm. Stansfield Turner) turned to a woman reputed to have psychic powers. As told by Carter, "she gave some latitude and longitude figures. We focused our satellite cameras on that point and the plane was there." Independently, Turner himself also has admitted the Agency's use of a remote viewer (in this case, Pat Price).[9] And recently, in a segment taped for the British television series Equinox [22], Maj. Gen. Ed Thompson, Assistant Chief of Staff for Intelligence, U.S. Army (1977-1981), volunteered "I had one or more briefings by SRI and was impressed.... The decision I made was to set up a small, in-house, low-cost effort in remote viewing…

Finally, a recent unclassified report [23] prepared for the CIA by the American Institutes for Research (AIR), concerning a remote viewing effort carried out under a DIA program called Star Gate (discussed in detail elsewhere in this volume), cites the roles of the CIA and DIA in the history of the program, including acknowledgment that a cadre of full-time government employees used remote viewing techniques to respond to tasking from operational military organizations. [10]

As information concerning the various programs spawned by intelligence-community interest is released, and the dialog concerning their scientific and social significance is joined, the results are certain to be hotly debated. Bearing witness to this fact are the companion articles in this volume by Ed May, Director of the SRI and SAIC programs since 1985, and by Jessica Utts and Ray Hyman, consultants on the AIR evaluation cited above. These articles address in part the AIR study. That study, limited in scope to a small fragment of the overall program effort, resulted in a conclusion that although laboratory research showed statistically significant results, use of remote viewing in intelligence gathering was not warranted.

# Evidential Details

Regardless of one's a priori position, however, an unimpassioned observer cannot help but attest to the <u>following fact</u>. Despite the ambiguities inherent in the type of exploration covered in these programs, the integrated results appear to provide <u>unequivocal evidence</u> of a human capacity to access events remote in space and time, however falteringly, by some cognitive process not yet understood. My years of involvement as a research manager in these programs have left me with the conviction that this fact must be taken into account in any attempt to develop an unbiased picture of the structure of reality.

# Footnotes

1 - One example being the release of documents that are the subject of this report - see the memoir by Russell Targ.

2 - Since the reputation of the intelligence services is mixed among members of the general populace, I have on occasion been challenged as to why I would agree to cooperate with the CIA or other elements of the intelligence community in this work. My answer is simply that as a result of my own previous exposure to this community I became persuaded that war can almost always be traced to a failure in intelligence, and that therefore the strongest weapon for peace is good intelligence.

3 - This result was published by us in advance of the ring's discovery [9].

4 - Editor's footnote added here: COTR - Contracting Officer's Technical Representative.

5 - An NSA listening post at the Navy's Sugar Grove facility, according to intelligence-community chronicler Bamford [15]

6 - DIA - Defense Intelligence Agency. The CIA dropped out as a major player in the mid-seventies due to pressure on the Agency (unrelated to the RV Program) from the Church-Pike Congressional Committee.

7 - See also the contribution by Ed May elsewhere in this volume concerning his experiences from 1985 on during his tenure as Director.

8 - For example, one application of this technique yielded not only a published, statistically significant result, but also a return of $26,000 in 30 days in the silver futures market [21].

9 - The direct quote is given in Targ's contribution elsewhere in this volume.

10 - "From 1986 to the first quarter of FY 1995, the DoD para-normal psychology program received more than 200 tasks from operational military organizations requesting that the program staff apply a paranormal psychological technique know (sic) as "remote viewing" (RV) to attain information unavailable from other sources."[23]

# References

[1] "CIA Statement on 'Remote Viewing," CIA Public Affairs Office, 6 September 1995.

[2] Harold E. Puthoff and Russell Targ, "Perceptual Augmentation Techniques," SRI Progress Report No. 3 (31 Oct. 1974) and Final Report (1 Dec. 1975) to the CIA,

covering the period January 1974 through February 1975, the second year of the program. This effort was funded at the level of $149,555.

[3] H. E. Puthoff, "Toward a Quantum Theory of Life Process," unpubl proposal, Stanford Research Institute (1972).

[4] H. E. Puthoff and R. Targ, "Physics, Entropy and Psychokine-sis," in Proc. Conf. Quantum Physics and Parapsychology (Gen-eva, Switzerland); (New York: Parapsychology Foundation, 1975).

[5] Documented in "Paraphysics R&D - Warsaw Pact (U)," DST-1810S-202-78, Defense Intelligence Agency (30 March 1978).

[6] R. Targ and H. E. Puthoff, "Information Transfer under Conditions of Sensory Shielding," Nature 252, 602 (1974).

[7] H. E. Puthoff and R. Targ, "A Perceptual Channel for Information Transfer over Kilometer Distances: Historical Perspective and Recent Research," Proc. IEEE 64, 329 (1976).

[8] H. E. Puthoff, R. Targ and E. C. May, "Experimental Psi Research: Implications for Physics," in The Role of Consciousness in the Physical World", edited by R. G. Jahn (AAAS Selected Symposium 57, Westview Press, Boulder, 1981).

[9] R. Targ and H. E. Puthoff, Mind Reach (Delacorte Press, New York, 1977).

[10] J. P. Bisaha and B. J. Dunne, "Multiple Subject and Long-Distance Precognitive Remote Viewing of Geographical Locations," in Mind at Large, edited by C. T. Tart, H. E. Puthoff and R. Targ (Praeger, New York, 1979), p. 107.

[11] B. J. Dunne and J. P. Bisaha, "Precognitive Remote Viewing in the Chicago Area: a Replication of the Stanford Experiment," J. Parapsychology 43, 17 (1979).

[12] R. G. Jahn, "The Persistent Paradox of Psychic Phenomena: An Engineering Perspective," Proc. IEEE 70, 136 (1982).

[13] R. G. Jahn and B. J. Dunne, "On the Quantum Mechanics of Consciousness with Application to Anomalous Phenomena," Found. Phys. 16, 721 (1986).

[14] R. G. Jahn and B. J. Dunne, Margins of Reality (Harcourt, Brace and Jovanovich, New York, 1987).

[15] J. Bamford, The Puzzle Palace (Penguin Books, New York, 1983) pp. 218-222.

[16] R. Targ, P. Cole and H. E. Puthoff, "Techniques to Enhance Man/ Machine Communication," Stanford Research Institute Final Report on NASA Project NAS7-100 (August 1974).

[17] R. Targ, E. C. May, H. E. Puthoff, D. Galin and R. Ornstein, "Sensing of Remote EM Sources (Physiological Correlates)," SRI Intern'l Final Report on Naval Electronics Systems Command Project N00039-76-C-0077, covering the period November 1975 - to October 1976 (April 1978).

[18] H. E. Puthoff, "Feasibility Study on the Vulnerability of the MPS System to RV Detection Techniques," SRI Internal Report, 15 April 1979; revised 2 May 1979.

[19] H. E. Puthoff, "Calculator-Assisted Psi Amplification," Research in Parapsychology 1984, edited by Rhea White and J. Solfvin (Scarecrow Press, Metuchen, NJ, 1985), p. 48.

[20] H. E. Puthoff, "Calculator-Assisted Psi Amplification II: Use of the Sequential-Sampling Technique as a Variable-Length Majority-Vote Code," Research in Parapsychology 1985, edited by D. Wei-ner and D. Radin (Scarecrow Press, Metuchen, NJ, 1986), p. 73.

[21] H. E. Puthoff, "ARV (Associational Remote Viewing) Applica-tions," Research in Parapsychology 1984, edited by Rhea White and J. Solfvin (Scarecrow Press, Metuchen, NJ, 1985), p. 121.

[22] "The Real X-Files", Independent Channel 4, England (27 August 1995); to be

shown in the U.S. on the Discovery Channel.

[23] M. D. Mumford, A. M. Rose and D. Goslin, "An Evaluation of Remote Viewing: Research and Applications", American Institutes for Research (September 29, 1995).

[The footnotes are to facilitate a greater understanding of Remote Viewing pioneers, but are not original. Dr. Puthoff's text was not altered.]

# Targeted Reading

This list was compiled to help people search
for media from members of the military program.

McMoneagle, Joseph W.
- *Mind Trek;* Hampton Roads, 1993
- *The Ultimate Time Machine*; Hampton Roads, 1998
- *Remote Viewing Secrets*; Hampton Roads, 2000
- *The Stargate Chronicles*; Hampton Roads, 2002
- *Memoirs of a Psychic Spy: The Remarkable Life of U. S. Government Remote Viewer 001*; Hampton Roads, 2006

Buchanan, Leonard
- *The Seventh Sense – The Secrets of Remote Viewing as Told by a "Psychic Spy" for the U.S. Military*; Paraview Pocket Books, 2003
- *Remote Viewing Methods - Remote Viewing and Remote Influencing*; DVD, 2004

Smith, Paul H.
- *Reading the Enemy's Mind - Inside Stargate - America's Psychic Espionage Program*; Tor non-fiction, 2005

Morehouse, David A.
- *Psychic Warrior – Inside the CIA's Stargate Program: The True Story of a Soldiers Espionage and Awakening*; St Martin's Press, 1996
- *Nonlethal Weapons: War Without Death;* Praeger Publishers, 1996
- *Remote Viewing: The Complete User's Manual for Coordinate Remote Viewing*; Sounds True Publishers, 2011

Atwater, F. Holmes
- *Captain of My Ship, Master of My Soul: Living with Guidance;* Hampton Roads Publishing, 2001 Puthoff, Harold E. with Targ, Russell

- *Mind Reach - Scientists Look at Psychic Abilities*; Delacorte, 1977 & New World Library, 2004

Swann, Ingo
- *To Kiss the Earth Goodbye;* Hawthorne, New York, 1975
- Star Fire, Dell non-fiction, 1978
- *Everybody's Guide to Natural ESP: Unlocking the Extrasensory Power of Your Mind;* Jeremy P. Tharcher Imprint, 1991
- *Your Nostradamus Factor*; Fireside Press, 1993
- *Remote Viewing & ESP from the Inside Out*; DVD

Targ, Russell
- *Mind Race: Understanding and Using Psychic Abilities*, with Keith Harary; Ballantine Books, 1984
- *Miracles of Mind: Exploring Nonlocal Consciousness and Spiritual Healing*; New World Library, 1999
- *Limitless Mind: A Guide to Remote Viewing and Transformation of Consciousness*; New World Library, 2004

## Other Resources

- Schnabel, Jim – *Remote Viewers: The Secret History of America's Psychic Spies*; Dell–non-fiction, 1997

- McRae, Ronald – *Mind Wars: The true story of Government Research into the Military Potential of Psychic Weapons*; St Martin's Press, 1984

- Moreno, Jonathon D. - *Mind Wars: Brain Science and the Military in the 21$^{st}$ Century*; Bellevue Literary Press, 2012

- Radin, Dean - *Entangled Minds: Extrasensory Experiences in a Quantum Reality*, Paraview Pocket Books, 2006

- Gruber, Elmar – *Psychic Wars – Parapsychology in Espionage – and Beyond*; Blandford, London, 1999

- Brown, Courtney - *Remote Viewing* - Farsight Press, 2005

# Additional Taskings

**Ötzal Alps - Italian-Austrian border ~ 3,300 BC** – Follow the trail of Europe's archeological "show of the century." Learn the whereabouts of **Ötzi the Iceman**'s unknown home camp and why he died alone high in the mountains which the Press incorrectly regards as a Neolithic crime scene. The book includes remote viewing maps, implement drawings with an undiscovered tool, his home, and the world's only real time portrait considered significant enough for the Museum in Bolzano, Italy to request for Ötzi's 20th Anniversary exhibit. Interwoven with scientific quotations, this account includes specifics on his tribal life. It is also the only book with **Ötzi's previously unknown course through the mountains** using modern Alpine trail numbers. Learn of his violent death's true cause which has recently become the more accepted version.

**RMS Titanic - North Atlantic - April, 1912** – In the first book to appear since the revelations of the 2nd Officer's grand-daughter, review the evidential details substantiating alleged **crow's nest irregularities** as *Titanic* bore down on the ice. Then, move to a resolution regarding **Captain E. J. Smith**'s final actions in his previously unknown non-drowning **death**. The book includes conformational Disaster Hearings testimony and McMoneagle's detailed artifact drawings whose shapes were only confirmed through future ocean salvage. Read History's only narrative of the last 20 minutes as the ship prepared to take over +1500 terrified passengers down into frigid black waters at 2:18 am.

**Civil War Special, State of Maryland - September, 1862** – Considered an unsolvable whodunit this little known but most significant mystery in America's Civil War resolves who lost Confederate General Robert E. Lee's top secret *Special Order 191*. The result was the battles of South Mountain and Harper's Ferry, which led directly to the bloodiest day in American History at Antietam Creek. The result was the timing of the Emancipation Proclamation and Europe's decision not to recognize the Confederacy, With information from the National Park Service, the book provides aerial maps and reveals **the unknown who, why, when, where and how** these orders found their way into the Union's Eastern Theater Commander's tent. The book also provides the world's first clinical explanation about General George McClellan's often discussed psychological problems.

**Last Stand Hill - Little Big Horn Battlefield, Montana - June, 1876** – This is History's only view of **General George Armstrong Custer's** last stand from the winners - and losers - perspectives. Read about Chief Sitting Bull's and Custer's battle thoughts. Finally learn of the true cause of his death and the reasons his body is likely not in his tomb at West Point. You'll get remote viewing generated battle maps with a drawing of Custer's last fighting stance, a near death facial close-up drawing, and, the actual wound that took him down. And since he was never photographed, the **world's only color portrait of Indian War Chief *Crazy Horse*** is included.

**Execution Square - Rouen, France - May, 1431** – Go to the stake in the market square for the burning of the military heroine lost in the mists of time - **Joan of Arc**. Recounted are her military successes, capture, the political intrigues and some trial excerpts. A detailed medieval architectural description of Rouen's town square, as Joan looked out at it, is included. McMoneagle's renowned artwork documents the scene as she was chained to the burning scaffold (not a stake), and includes the **world's only portrait of the heroine** who went on to become a Saint.

**Streets of Whitechapel – Whitechapel, London, England – Fall, 1888** – A human energy comparison from suspect James Maybrick's Liverpool death bed, to an actual **Ripper murder in progress.** This book provides the world's only portraits of Jack and one of his apprehensive victims (Elizabeth Stride) as they spoke moments before her death. Get inside Jack's head and learn of his motivations. The book includes a draftsmen's drawing of his mysterious knife, his hat, and exposes why this criminal is supposed to remain a mystery.

Each book has a military intelligence level report providing the Evidential Details you'll need to resolve all of these mysteries.

# Princess Diana References

[i] McMoneagle, Joseph W., *Remote Viewing Secrets – A Handbook*; Hampton Roads Publishing Company, Inc. 2000 p. xv

[ii] McMoneagle, Joseph W., *The Stargate Chronicles*; Hampton Roads Publishing Company, Inc. 2002 p. 182

[iii] Simmons, Simone, *Diana – The Secret Years* with Susan Hill; Ballantine Books 1998 p.120

[iv] Delorm, Rene, *Diana & Dodi - A Love Story - By the Butler Who Saw Their Romance Blossom*, with Barry Fox and Nadine Taylor; Tallfellow Press 1998 p.144

[v] Anderson, Christopher, *The Day Diana Died;* William Morrow and Company 1998 p.114

[vi] Anderson; p.113

[vii] Delorm; p.154

[viii] ibid; p.154

[ix] The Learning Channel Presentation - *Princess Diana*; A Fulcrum Production; a Granada Presentation for ITV 1998; hereafter referred to as *TLC*

[x] Delorm; p.155

[xi] Anderson; p.99

[xii] ibid; p.166

[xiii] Sancton, Thomas and Scott MacLeod, *Death of a Princess - The Investigation*; St. Martin's Press 1998 p.157

[xiv] Delorm; p.157

[xv] ibid; p.158

[xvi] Spoto, Donald, *Diana - The Last Year,*; Harmony Books 1997 p. 171

[xvii] Sanction; p.158-9

[xviii] TLC - Mohammed Al-Fayed interview

[xix] Junor, Penny, *Charles - Victim or Villain*; Harper Collins Publishers 1998; p.18

[xx] Sanction; p.167

[xxi] Final Report - Paris Prosecutor's Office; Head of the Prosecution Department at Courts of the First Instance; Examining Magistrates Hervé Stephan and Christine Devidal

[xxii] *TLC* - documentary information

[xxiii] *TLC* - interview with Dr. Martin Skinner.

[xxiv] Anderson; p.191

[xxv] Interview with Mohammed Al Fayed as per his internet site address: www.alfayed.com/indexie4.html, as published to the Internet on October 25, 1998

[xxvi] Spoto; p.172

[xxvii] Sanction; p 251

[xxviii] ibid; p. 6

[xxix] *Newsweek* Magazine; September 8, 1997; p. 33

[xxx] ibid; p. 241

[xxxi] Buchanan, Lyn, *The Seventh Sense*, Paraview Pocket Books, 2003, p. 190

[xxxii] Sanction; p. 17

[xxxiii] ibid; p.17 - 18

[xxxiv] Junor; p. 20

[xxxv] Spoto; p.180

[xxxvi] Junor; p. 22

[xxxvii] *French Final Accident Report* – Conclusionary Statement section

[xxxviii] Lyall, Sarah; New York Times; December 15, 2008

# Amelia Earhart References

xxxix Goerner, Fred, *The Search for Amelia Earhart*; Doubleday & Company 1966; p. 74

xl Putnam, George Palmer, *Soaring Wings - A Biography of Amelia Earhart*; Hartcourt, Brace and Company, Inc; 1939; p. 290

xli *Faheys-Ships and Aircraft of the US Fleet* - War Edition

xlii *Putnam*; p. 291

xliii Schnabel, Jim, *Remote Viewers: The Secret History of America's Psychic Spies*; Dell Publishing a division of the Bantam Doubleday Dell Publishing Group, New York 1997; p. 229

xliv Wikipedia, the free encyclopedia - Lae Airport Papua New Guinea page.

xlv *Putnam*; p. 274

xlvi *Goerner*; p. 34

xlvii *Ibid*; p. 30

xlviii *Ibid*; p. 30

xlix *Putnam*; p. 294

l Carroll, Andrew *Letters of a Nation – A Collection of Extraordinary American Letters*; Kodansha International Limited 1997, p. 379

li Oral History Collection, *The Reminiscences of Murial Earhart Morrissey;* Columbia University1960; p. 7

lii *Putnam*; p. 291

liii *Western* Union telegram stamped 03:04 a.m., July 2, 1937, to the Press Tribune, 424 Thirteenth Street, Oakland, CA. archived at The Amelia Earhart Digital Collection at Purdue University Libraries, West Lafayette, IN.

liv Lovell, Mary S. *The Sound of Wings - The Life of Amelia Earhart*; St. Martin's Press 1989; p. 277; see also Pellegreno, Ann Holtgren, *World Flight – The Earhart Trail*; The Iowa State University Press/Ames; 1971 as source material.

lv Ibid; p. 277

lvi Chater, Eric H., General Manager, Guinea Airways Limited; report to M.E. Griffin, Placer Management Limited, San Francisco, California, dated Lae, New Guinea July 25, 1937.

lvii *Goerner*; p. 35

lviii http://www.cia.gov/cia/publications/factbook/geos/hq/html

lix Butler, Susan, *East to the Dawn – the Life of Amelia Earhart*; Addison Wesley Longman1997; p.408

lx *The Chater Report*;

lxi Pellegreno, Ann Holtgren, *World Flight – The Earhart Trail*; The Iowa State University Press/Ames; 1971; p. 4

lxii Ibid; p. 406

lxiii *Butler*; p. 318

lxiv http://easytide.ukho.gov.uk/easytide/easytide/showprediction.aspx

lxv As per a discussion with Archeologist Tom King at Benedictine University in Atchison, Kansas, July 21, 2018.

lxvi http://tighar.org/Publications/TTracks/12_2/obj11.html as shown in 2016

lxvii All United States Air Force National Museum staff quotations are referenced from The TIGHAR Group's web site - The Riddle of Artifact #2-2-V-1, Earhart Project Research Bulletin #71, dated May 22, 2014

lxviii *Goerner*; p. 36

lxix *Ibid*; p. 36

lxx Brink, Randall, *Lost Star – The Search for Amelia Earhart*, W.W. Norton & Company1993; p. 144

lxxi Edited communication between Comfrandiv and Comhawsec; 1010Z; July 6, 1937 lxxii *Lovell*; p. 240

lxxiii *Lovell*; p. 240 - Purdue University – Both quotes Amelia Earhart's archived scrapbooks preserving articles clipped from the *Cleveland Press* and the New York *Daily Mirror*, Feb.16, 1937

lxxiv Both quotes National Archives Research Agency

lxxv United States Navy Archives; George Putnam to Secretary of Commerce Daniel Roper; Cablegram dated July 23, 1937

lxxvi *Putnam*; p. 37

lxxvii As per my discussions with Granddaughter Cynthia Putnam at the Amelia Earhart Birthplace Museum in Atchison, Kansas on July 15, 2017.

lxxviii Both references from Archaeological Sciences Magazine, Pamela J. Cross & Richard Wright - *The Nikumaroro bones identification controversy: First-hand examination versus evaluation by proxy — Amelia Earhart found or still missing?*, University of Bradford, Bradford, UK and Emeritus Professor of Anthropology, University of Sydney respectively.

lxxix United States Department of Justice File 62-48646

lxxx U.S. Navy; Senior Aviator Lambrecht Report – *Aircraft Search for Earhart Plane;* 16 July 1937 to the Chief of the Bureau of Aeronautics

lxxxi Eric Bevington's Journal – entry dated Wednesday, October 13, 1937

lxxxii Laxton, Paul B.; *Nikumaroro - The Journal of the Polynesian Society,* June/ September 1951

lxxxiii Isaac, L., 1941b. 22a. February 11, 1941. Telegram (not numbered) from Isaac to Gallagher. TIGHAR 32 (April 4, 1941. http://tighar.org/Projects/ Earhart/Archives/Documents/ Bones_ Chronology3.html).

lxxxiv ibid

lxxxv TIGHAR's Ameliapedia Web Site, page, *Niku III – Once and For All*

lxxxvi TIGHAR Web Site, quoted May 28, 2013

lxxxvii http://tighar.org/Projects/Earhart/Archives/Research/ResearchPapers/Branden-burg/signalcatalog.html

lxxxviii The Washington Post via MSN News 9/16/16

lxxxix Wolford, Josh - WebProNews Science Page; June 2, 2013

xc Series of quotations from Department of State documents - Case No. F-2012-29756 dated 08/07/2015

xci Smith, Len Young and Roberson, G. Gale – Legal definition of Fraud; Business Law, Uniform Commercial Code, Third Edition; West Publishing Company, 1971, p.198

Made in United States
Orlando, FL
26 August 2025

64312648R00098